CLASSICAL MYTH

A TREASURY OF GREEK AND ROMAN LEGENDS, ART, AND HISTORY

This edition published in 2007 by:

Chartwell Books, Inc.
A Division of Book Sales, Inc.
114 Northfield Avenue
Edison, New Jersey 08837

A Marshall Edition
Conceived, edited and designed by Marshall Editions
The Old Brewery
6 Blundell Street
London N7 9BH, UK
www.quarto.com

ISBN-13: 978-0-7858-2350-6
ISBN-10: 0-7858-2350-6

Originated in Hong Kong by Modern Age
Printed and bound in China by Midas Printing Limited

10 9 8 7 6 5 4 3 2 1

Publisher: Richard Green
Commissioning editor: Claudia Martin
Art director: Ivo Marloh
Picture manager: Veneta Bullen
Design and editorial: Tall Tree Ltd.
Production: Anna Pauletti

Previous page: The Emperor Hadrian (76–138 C.E.) had this magnificent villa complex constructed in the second century C.E.
Opposite: This stone head was carved in Italy in c. 257 C.E. and depicts Jupiter, the king of the gods. He was known as Zeus to the Greeks.
This page and opposite: The ruins of the forum, ancient Rome's central public square, still stand in the city today.

CLASSICAL MYTH

A TREASURY OF GREEK AND ROMAN LEGENDS, ART, AND HISTORY

JANE BINGHAM

CHARTWELL
BOOKS, INC.

CONTENTS

ANCIENT HEROES

ROMAN HEROES

INTRODUCTION

The group of stories known as the classical myths were first written down by the ancient Greeks and Romans—the joint creators of what is known as "classical" civilization. But these powerful stories have an even older origin. They were first told in the Mediterranean region over four thousand years ago, and were passed down through the generations by word of mouth. Centuries later, these stories were recorded by some of the greatest writers of the classical world.

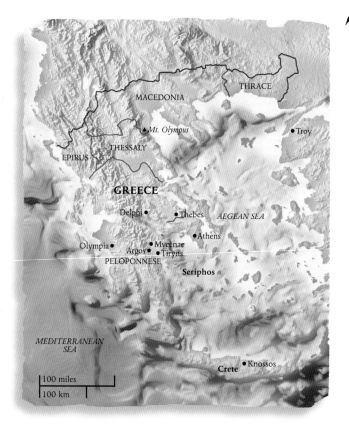

The classical myths have their origins in the earliest civilizations of the Mediterranean: the remarkable cultures of the Minoans and the Mycenaeans. The Minoans flourished on the island of Crete from around 2000 B.C.E. They built vast royal palaces for their kings, and worshipped powerful goddesses. Around 1600 B.C.E., the Minoan culture began to decline, but by this time another civilization was emerging. The Mycenaeans of central Greece were great builders, warriors, and goldsmiths. These two early civilizations provided the setting for many of the legends of the Greeks and Romans.

Left: The classical myths began with stories told on the islands and lands around the Mediterranean Sea. These ancient stories were recorded by later Greek and Roman writers, who added some new elements of their own.

THE WORLD OF THE GREEKS

The Mycenaean civilization had collapsed by around 1200 B.C.E. There then followed a long period, sometimes known as the Dark Ages, when the population of the region declined and the Greeks lost the art of writing. Then, around 800 B.C.E., a new culture emerged. This was the start of the civilization of ancient Greece. The time that historians consider to be the early period of Greek history lasted from around 800 to 500 B.C.E. and is known today as the Archaic Period. During this time, the Greeks began to settle in lands all around the Mediterranean Sea. They set up small independent kingdoms, with their own rulers and armies, known as city-states.

Gradually, the city-state of Athens emerged as the most powerful of all. From c. 500 to 350 B.C.E., Athens dominated ancient Greece. Known as the Classical Period, this was a time when literature, art, and architecture flourished. However, around 350 B.C.E., the kingdom of Macedonia, in the north of Greece, began to dominate the rest of Greece and, in 338 B.C.E., King Philip of Macedon became the ruler of the Greeks. Philip was succeeded by his son, Alexander the Great, who won a large empire for the Greeks, including lands in Persia and Egypt.

Alexander's death in 323 B.C.E. marked the start of the final period of ancient Greek history, the so-called Hellenistic Period, which lasted from 323 to c. 30 B.C.E. During this time, Greek culture was widespread but strongly influenced by the Persians and the Egyptians. Gradually, the Greeks lost control of their empire, and by 146 B.C.E. the Romans had conquered all of Greece. This was the end of the ancient Greek world, but the Romans copied many aspects of Greek culture, and adopted their ancient legends.

THE ROMANS AND THEIR EMPIRE

The first Romans were a tribe called the Latins, who settled in central Italy around 1000 B.C.E. The Latins built villages on the banks of the Tiber River and, by the eighth century B.C.E., a small town had begun to emerge. From this town, the city of Rome developed, and its people became known as Romans. By 264 B.C.E., the Romans controlled all of Italy, and they began to conquer neighboring lands.

Rome was governed by a group of elected men known as the Senate until, in 27 B.C.E., the leader Augustus seized total power over all the Roman lands, becoming the first Roman emperor (from the Latin for "supreme commander"). The Roman Empire grew unstoppably and, by 117 C.E., it had reached its greatest extent. It stretched 2,500 miles (4,000 km) from east to west, and was home to more than 50 million people. Everywhere the Romans conquered, they built fine cities and introduced their language, laws, and religion.

Right: Augustus (63 B.C.E.–14 C.E.) was the first in a line of emperors who ruled the Roman Empire for 500 years. Thanks to the Romans, the classical legends became well known all over the ancient world.

However, by the year 400 C.E., barbarian tribes had begun to attack the empire's tottering defenses and claim its lands. In 476 C.E., the Germanic chieftain Odoacer (o-doe-ak-a) seized Rome and took control of Italy. Historians consider this event to mark the fall of the Roman Empire.

A LASTING LEGACY

Although the classical world came to an end almost 2,000 years ago, its legacy has never disappeared. For centuries, people have been influenced by classical ideas, laws, and methods of government. Greek and Roman art and architecture have been copied all over the world, and the myths of the Greeks and Romans are still remembered today. The adventures of the ancient gods, monsters, and heroes have been told in many forms—poems, storybooks, statues, paintings, and movies—but they have never lost their power to surprise, fascinate, and terrify.

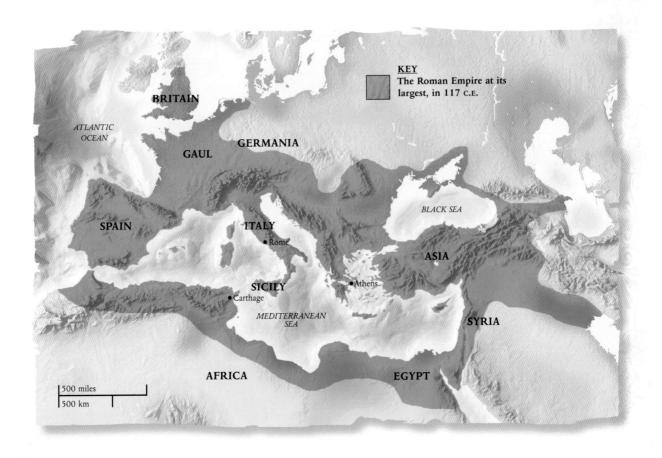

KEY
The Roman Empire at its largest, in 117 C.E.

Many classical creation stories are set in real places. In one legend, the young god Zeus carries a sacred stone to Delphi in central Greece. The Greeks built the Shrine of Apollo at Delphi to mark the spot where Zeus set down his stone.

In the Beginning

Like all civilizations, the Greeks and Romans had a set of stories to explain how the world began. These ancient myths tell how the earth was formed and how the gods were born. They follow the rise of the god Zeus and his battles for power, and describe how humans first arrived in the world.

The Greek creation stories were first written down by the poet Hesiod in the eighth century B.C.E., but they had been told for centuries before this. Scholars have discovered that the Greek legends share many elements with the creation stories of other civilizations, especially those of ancient Babylon and Assyria in what is today known as the Middle East. Later, the Greek creation myths were adopted by the Romans and have been retold ever since. Like the myths of other civilizations, these myths aim to answer some very big questions: How was the earth formed? How did human beings arrive on the earth? Why is there evil in the world?

THE AGE OF THE GODS

In the beginning there was a deep nothingness known as Chaos. Then, out of this dark, empty state, two powerful beings slowly emerged. One was Gaia (JEE-ah), the vast, motherly goddess of the earth. The other was Tartarus, the gloomy ruler of a deep underground kingdom. From these two beings, the world began to take shape.

Gaia and Tartarus were not alone for long. The next god to emerge out of Chaos was Eros, the god of love. With the help of Eros, Gaia created a husband for herself. He was handsome Uranus, the god of the sky.

Every night, Uranus covered Gaia with his heavenly cloak and together they had many children. First, Gaia gave birth to twelve giant children, six male and six female, known as the Titans. Later, she had six more sons who were truly terrifying to look at. First there were the Cyclopes, three massive giants, each with a single eye in the middle of his forehead. Then came three monsters, each with fifty heads and a hundred hands.

Uranus hated the sight of his children, and he treated them cruelly. Meanwhile, urged on by their mother, the Titans plotted to overthrow their father. In the end it was Cronus, the youngest of the Titans, who dared to attack Uranus. His father fled, nursing his wounds, and Cronus became the new ruler of the earth and sky.

A DANGEROUS FATHER

Cronus married one of the other Titans, called Rhea, and together they had five children. But Cronus had been warned that one of his children would kill him. So each time Rhea gave birth, Cronus snatched up the baby and swallowed it whole. This made Rhea distraught, and she appealed to her mother Gaia for help. When Rhea was expecting her sixth child, Gaia carried her off to the island of Crete. There, Rhea's son was born, far away from his dangerous father.

As soon as the baby was born, Gaia hid him in a mountain cave. Then she took a stone from the mountainside and wrapped it in baby clothes. Rhea returned to Cronus and offered him the bundle, which he gobbled up straight away. Cronus was convinced that he had seen the last of his children. But little did he know that his youngest son, who was called Zeus, was preparing to become the greatest god of all.

While he was growing up on Crete, Zeus learned all about his father's cruelty. He discovered the terrible fate of his brothers and sisters. He also learned that Cronus had imprisoned some of Gaia's children. The Cyclopes and the many-headed giants were locked in the depths of the kingdom of Tartarus.

THE REVENGE OF ZEUS

As soon as he was old enough, Zeus decided to take revenge on his father. With the help of a Titan, he prepared a magic potion. Then he traveled to Cronus's court, disguised as a servant.

Below: Gaia is often known as Mother Earth. In this Roman carving, from the second century C.E., she is shown as a caring mother. The headless figure on the left is Demeter, the goddess of the harvest.

THE OLYMPIC GAMES

One of the ancient Greeks' most sacred sites was the city of Olympia, in southwest Greece. There is evidence that the Greeks began building temples on this site as early as the eighth century B.C.E. One of these early buildings was an altar to Zeus.

Around the year 776 B.C.E., the Greeks began to hold races at Olympia as part of a festival for Zeus. Gradually, these contests developed into the Olympic Games, and by the sixth century B.C.E., people from all over the Greek world

were flocking to Olympia to attend the games. The ancient Olympics were held every four years and featured five days of sporting events, including running, boxing, and chariot racing. The games began with a ceremony to Zeus, and most of the third day was devoted to honoring the god.

Right: This vase painting of an Olympic athlete (c. 500 B.C.E.) probably depicts a pentathlon champion. He holds a discus in his left hand. The painting also shows a marking stick for the long jump and two curved stone weights, which athletes swung behind them in the long jump to help them jump further.

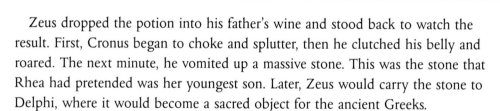

Zeus dropped the potion into his father's wine and stood back to watch the result. First, Cronus began to choke and splutter, then he clutched his belly and roared. The next minute, he vomited up a massive stone. This was the stone that Rhea had pretended was her youngest son. Later, Zeus would carry the stone to Delphi, where it would become a sacred object for the ancient Greeks.

Then Cronus vomited up the rest of his children—his sons Poseidon and Hades (hay-dees), and his daughters Hera, Hestia, and Demeter. All five children were fully grown adults and powerful gods and goddesses. They joined their brother Zeus as the new rulers of the world.

This was not the end of Zeus's revenge. His next step was to free the six giant brothers from the terrible pit of Tartarus. After many years of darkness and despair, the giants finally stumbled into the light. They were so happy to be free that they became loyal servants of Zeus.

THE GODS OF OLYMPIA

Zeus created a kingdom for the gods at the top of Mount Olympus, in northern Greece. This country of the gods was known as Olympia, and the gods who lived there were called the Olympians.

In addition to Zeus and his brothers and sisters, the Olympians included the gods Apollo, Ares (air-ees), and Hermes (herm-ees), and the goddesses Athena, Artemis, and Aphrodite.

Right: The Spanish artist Francisco Goya depicted Cronus as a savage and brutal giant in his *Cronus Devouring One of his Children* (1820–1823).

Right: All the gods and goddesses joined in the battle against the Titans. This Greek carving shows Apollo and Artemis challenging the Titans (right). It was carved in Delphi around 525 B.C.E.

After the Cyclopes were released from the pit of Tartarus, they presented Zeus and his brothers with gifts. Poseidon, the god of the sea, was given a trident to help him rule the waves. Hades, the god of the underworld, was presented with a helmet that made him invisible. Mighty Zeus, the ruler of the gods, received the gift of thunder and lightning. Whenever he was angry, Zeus could hurl a thunderbolt down from Mount Olympus.

Armed with these special weapons, the gods were very powerful. But they faced a terrible enemy. Across the plain of Thessaly from Mount Olympus was another high mountain. This was Mount Othrys, the home of the Titans and their mother Gaia. The Titans were bitterly jealous of Zeus and the Olympians. With cruel Cronus as their leader, they were determined to wage war on the gods.

WAR WITH THE TITANS

For ten long years, the gods and the Titans fought each other on the plain of Thessaly. The battles were long and fierce, but no clear winner emerged. Eventually, Zeus decided to ask the many-headed giants for help. They were still angry with Cronus for keeping them imprisoned, and they charged off wildly across the plain.

When the giants reached Mount Othrys, they used their hundred hands to throw huge rocks at the Titans' palace. All the gods joined in the battle, and even mighty Zeus hurled

Classical Myth

thunderbolts at his enemies. The Titans fought back fiercely, and their battle cries could be heard from the top of Mount Olympus to the depths of Tartarus. All over the earth, oceans boiled and mountains trembled with the force of the fighting, but in the end the Titans were defeated.

After his victory, Zeus bound the Titans in chains and threw them into the pit of Tartarus. But not all the Titans ended up in prison. The giant Atlas was condemned to stand forever at the edge of the earth, holding up the sky on his massive shoulders. Zeus allowed Gaia to go free, but later this act of kindness led to serious trouble for him.

FIGHTING TYPHON

After the Titans were banished, there was a brief period of peace—until Gaia decided to have another child. This time the father was Tartarus, and their son was a terrifying creature known as Typhon. He had a hundred snakes for legs and a hundred heads that sometimes spoke in a bellow, sometimes in a roar, and sometimes in a hiss. This proud monster had one ambition: to rule the heavens and the earth.

When Zeus heard about Typhon's plans, he leaped down from Mount Olympus onto the creature's back. The god and the monster fought a violent battle. Typhon lashed out wildly with his snake legs, while Zeus used his thunderbolts to hammer the monster into the ground. After a vicious struggle, Zeus managed to overcome Typhon and hurled his body deep into Tartarus. There Typhon lay, twisting and turning far underground. Later, this restless monster was the cause of violent storms, known as typhoons.

THE GODS

The ancient Greeks had dozens of different gods. As well as Zeus and the Olympians—the twelve great gods who lived on Mount Olympus—there were many minor gods and goddesses who helped people in different aspects of their lives. The early Romans also worshipped numerous gods, who presided over the natural and human world. Over time, in addition to their native gods, the Romans also came to adopt many of the Greek gods and goddesses as their own.

Hermes

Hermes (or Mercury) was the messenger of the gods. With the help of his winged sandals, he flew swiftly between heaven and earth. This statue is a Roman copy of a famous Greek work, created by Lysippus around 300 B.C.E. The sculptor has emphasized the youthful, boyish nature of the god.

Poseidon

Poseidon (or Neptune) ruled the oceans. This second-century C.E. Roman mosaic shows him riding a chariot drawn by seahorses. It was made in the Roman colony of Tunisia.

MIXED RELIGIONS

As well as adopting the Greek gods, the Romans also identified existing Roman gods with their Greek counterparts. In this way, Jupiter, ruler of the Roman gods, became linked with Zeus and took on many of his characteristics and myths.

In both Greece and Rome, people worshipped the gods by praying to them and offering them gifts. These gifts could range from simple cakes and wine to sacrifices of animals. The most important gods had magnificent temples built in their honor. There, priests and priestesses made solemn offerings to giant statues.

Most Greek and Roman homes had their own shrine where the family met to pray. Roman families prayed to household spirits called *lares*, which protected their homes. By the end of the fourth century C.E., worship of the Roman gods had almost died out and Christianity was the official religion of the Roman Empire.

GUIDE TO THE GODS

Greek name	Roman name	
Zeus	Jupiter	king of the gods, god of the sky, thunder and lightning
Hera	Juno	queen of the gods, goddess of women and childbirth
Apollo	Apollo	god of the sun, music, healing, and prophecy
Artemis	Diana	goddess of the moon and of hunting
Aphrodite	Venus	goddess of love and beauty
Hermes	Mercury	messenger of the gods, and god of trade
Poseidon	Neptune	god of the sea
Hades	Pluto	god of the underworld
Athena	Minerva	goddess of science and wisdom, crafts, and war
Ares	Mars	god of war
Hestia	Vesta	goddess of the hearth
Demeter	Ceres	goddess of crops and harvests

Artemis

The Greek goddess Artemis was known as Diana by the Romans. This Roman painting of the goddess was made in Naples in the first century C.E. She was a skillful hunter and is often shown with her bow and arrow.

Zeus

Zeus (or Jupiter) was feared and respected because of his power over human lives. This colossal head of Zeus was made around 257 C.E. and is a Roman copy of a Greek statue.

THE FIRST HUMANS

Once Zeus had overcome his enemies, he settled down to enjoy life on Mount Olympus with his new wife, the great goddess Hera. The Olympians spent their time listening to music and feasting on ambrosia, the food of the gods. Yet in spite of all these pleasures, Zeus began to grow bored. He decided it was time to create some human beings.

Zeus had three attempts at making humans, and each time he made only men. First he made the men of the golden age who lived in paradise. They laughed and sang all day and did no work. Eventually, these men grew old and died, but their spirits continued to roam over the earth, keeping watch over later generations. Zeus's next creations were the men of the silver age. They were more like animals than men and wasted their time quarreling and fighting. Zeus realized these men would never change and destroyed them. The third set of humans were the men of the bronze age. They were more intelligent than the men of the silver age, but they still loved to fight. They spent their time making weapons, which they used to kill each other until they had all died out.

After his three attempts, Zeus was very discouraged. He was wondering whether the human race was a good idea, but decided to have one last try. This time, he was helped by a wise giant called Prometheus (pro-MEE-thee-us). Together they created the men of the heroic age. These men were the ancestors of the Greeks and Romans.

PROMETHEUS'S GIFT

Prometheus was a skilled potter who could mold figures from clay. When Zeus saw the tall, handsome men that Prometheus made, he was pleased with them and gave them the breath of life. Then Zeus set the men down on earth to see how they would manage for themselves.

Opposite: This seventeenth-century painting by Jan Cossiers shows Prometheus stealing fire. The courageous giant disobeyed mighty Zeus to provide humans with the gift of fire.

Life was very hard for the men of the heroic age. They had no knowledge of fire, so they were freezing cold and could only eat raw food. They were also unable to make any tools without fire.

Prometheus took pity on mankind and begged Zeus to give them the gift of fire, but the god refused. He was afraid that, once they had fire, men would become too powerful and challenge him.

Prometheus knew that Zeus would never change his mind, so he secretly made his way up to the top of Mount Olympus, where a fire always burned. He grabbed some glowing coals and pushed them into the hollow stalk of a fennel plant. Then he flew swiftly down to earth with his gift for men. When the humans realized all the things they could do with fire, they were delighted. At last they had the chance to become true heroes!

Prometheus did not just provide humans with fire: he also taught them many valuable skills. He showed them how to make pots, weapons, and tools. He also taught them how to make sacrifices to the gods. Zeus had demanded that men should offer most of whatever animals they killed to the gods. But Prometheus feared that this would mean that men would go hungry. He persuaded Zeus to accept just a part of each animal that was killed. Zeus agreed—on the condition that he should be allowed to choose the best part.

Crafty Prometheus divided the carcass of an ox into two piles. One pile was made up of all the meat and most of the fat. The other pile was waste: the innards and bones that were no good to eat. Prometheus stuffed the meat into the ox's hide, and wrapped the waste in some tasty-looking fat. When the two bundles were offered to Zeus, the god made the wrong choice. From then on, the gods always had to accept bones and innards for their sacrifice.

PUNISHING PROMETHEUS

Prometheus had managed to trick Zeus twice, but he could not escape the god's anger forever. One night, Zeus looked down from Mount Olympus and saw the fires of men. He realized that Prometheus had dared to disobey him and flew into a terrible rage. Zeus thought very hard about the best way to punish the giant. Then he gave orders that Prometheus should be chained to a cliff. Every day, a hungry eagle called Ethon, the offspring of the monster Typhon, would peck out the giant's liver. But every night Prometheus was healed so that he could suffer the same torture again the next day.

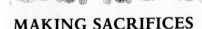

MAKING SACRIFICES

The ancient Greeks and Romans both performed animal sacrifices. These solemn ceremonies usually took place on an open-air altar in front of a temple. Oxen were the most common victims, but goats, sheep, pigs, and doves could all be sacrificed to the gods.

The sacrifice was performed by a priest or priestess who followed some basic rules. First, the animal was decorated with garlands and led to the altar. Then the priest slit its throat, while musicians played and female worshippers wailed and screamed. After this, the animal's organs and bones were removed and burned on a fire so that their smoke could travel up to the gods. The rest of the meat was roasted and shared out in a feast for all the worshippers. Often, the priest would examine the animal's organs before they were burned. The patterns made by the organs were used by the priest to interpret the will of the gods.

Above: A Greek priestess prepares to sacrifice a sheep on a stone altar. She is accompanied by musicians and worshippers, and she holds a jug in her hand. The jug contains water, which is sprinkled over the animal's head before it is offered to the gods.

In the Beginning **23**

Left: The tragic figure of Pandora has fascinated artists for centuries. The British artist Dante Gabriel Rossetti painted this picture of Pandora in 1871. Like Eve in the Bible, she carries the blame for letting evil into the world.

After he had punished Prometheus, Zeus turned his attention to earth. He was furious that men had dared to use fire, so he decided to teach them a lesson. Up until that time, all the people on earth had been men, but now Zeus had a cunning plan. He would create a different sort of being and send her down to the earth to cause endless trouble in the world of men.

Classical Myth

Zeus commanded the god Hephaestus (hef-eye-stus) to model a girl from clay. Athena breathed life into her, Hermes taught her cunning and charm, and Aphrodite gave her grace and beauty. Then they led the girl, whose name was Pandora, to the great god Zeus.

PANDORA'S BOX

Zeus smiled at Pandora as he offered her a beautiful golden casket.

"This is a present for you," he said, "but you must never open it. The gods have given you everything that you could desire and you must be happy with what you have."

Before Pandora had time to reply, Hermes whisked her down to earth to meet her new husband, Epimetheus (ep-ee-MEE-thee-us). Hermes gave Epimetheus the key to Pandora's box and instructed him to keep it safe. Then he left the couple alone together.

Pandora was very happy with her life on earth, and at first she never thought about her casket. But, as time went by, she began to think about it more and more. She pestered Epimetheus to give her the key, and when he refused she became even more determined. Eventually, Pandora saw her chance. While her husband was sleeping, she silently eased the key off his belt.

Pandora carefully slid the key into the lock of her mysterious casket, but for a moment she hesitated. Why had Zeus insisted that she should never look inside? She considered not opening it after all, but then she was overcome by curiosity. Pandora lifted up the lid just a crack, and straight away she heard a wild, rushing sound. Out of the box swirled a damp, dark cloud which raced straight through the door and out into the world. The cloud was filled with all the things that make people suffer— sickness, hatred, greed, poverty, jealousy, and distrust—and all these evils were spreading throughout the earth. Desperately Pandora tried to close the lid, but it was much too late. From then on human beings would always have to struggle and would never be able to live perfect, happy lives.

Zeus had punished mankind cruelly, but his triumph was not complete. Pandora fearfully peered inside the box—and there, right at the bottom, she saw something beautiful. Quickly she slammed down the lid before it could escape. The beautiful thing Pandora saw was hope. By saving hope, she had made life bearable for human beings. As long as they had hope, they still had a reason to go on living.

Many legends give an explanation for things that happen in nature, such as snowfall, as seen here in Athens during winter. In the story of Hades and Persephone, Demeter, the goddess of harvests, is mourning and neglects her duty to warm the Earth, causing the people of Greece to suffer freezing cold each year.

Mortals and Immortals

After their first experiments with making mortals, the gods created many more human beings, and soon the world was filled with men and women. The immortals kept a careful watch over human lives. In particular, the gods liked to be sure that all the mortals knew their place. Anyone who grew too proud was punished severely, but virtuous mortals were rewarded. Sometimes the gods claimed a mortal boy or girl for themselves— but this almost always ended in tragedy.

Most of the myths in this chapter teach a lesson to over-confident mortals. Some of the stories also explain aspects of nature, such as the reason for echoes in the mountains or the cold weather in winter. But, whatever their purpose, all the legends involve a dramatic conflict as the ordinary human world is touched by the magic of the gods.

HADES AND PERSEPHONE

When Hades, the god of the underworld, fell in love with Persephone (per-SEF-oh-nee), he did not consider the reaction of her powerful mother. Persephone was the daughter of Demeter, the goddess of plants and crops, and Demeter's grief at the loss of her daughter had dramatic consequences for everyone living on earth.

Demeter was a caring mother who wanted the very best for her only daughter. While Persephone was still a tiny baby, Demeter took her to live on the Mediterranean island of Sicily. There Persephone grew up amid fertile fields, ripe olive groves, and vines heavy with grapes. The girl had many human friends for company. By the time she was seventeen, she had become a beautiful young woman who loved to spend her time outdoors, searching for rare flowers and plants.

Every morning, Persephone and her friends set out for the meadows, and every evening they returned with their arms full of flowers. But then, one dreadful day, her friends came back without Persephone. Choking back their tears, the girls told Demeter what had happened. One moment Persephone had been picking flowers, and the next the earth had opened up, and she had been sucked inside. The girls had caught a glimpse of a jet-black chariot with a solemn driver, and then Persephone had simply disappeared.

A DESPERATE SEARCH

Demeter was beside herself with worry. First she scoured every inch of the island, and then she began to trudge all over the earth, searching desperately for her daughter. All the time she was searching, Demeter thought of nothing but Persephone. She forgot to care for the plants and crops, and gradually everything on the earth began to wither and die. The weather became icy, and the nights grew longer. People could no longer grow food to feed themselves, but Demeter did not care. Why should she look after the earth when her beloved daughter was not there to enjoy it?

Just as it seemed that everything on earth would die, Demeter met Arethusa (a-reth-oos-a), a talking fountain who had once been an underground stream. Arethusa told Demeter that while she was flowing through the underworld she had spotted Hades with his beautiful queen. Hades' wife looked pale and sad, and she held a withered bunch of flowers in her hands. Could this be Demeter's missing daughter?

Demeter was convinced that Arethusa had seen Persephone, and she set off straight away for Mount Olympus. There, she demanded that Zeus should rescue her daughter without delay. Zeus agreed to send Hermes down to the underworld, but he reminded Demeter of Hades' one unbreakable rule. Anyone who had ever tasted the food of the dead had to stay in the underworld forever.

Hermes flew straight to the underworld, where he found Persephone wandering alone. He asked the queen a very important question: Had she eaten any food in Hades' kingdom? Persephone shook her head, and Hermes seized her hand. He was ready to escort her back to the land of the living.

Right: This Greek carving from the fifth century B.C.E. shows Hades and Persephone seated on their throne in the underworld. Persephone holds some wheat stalks, symbols of the harvest, while Hades carries a pomegranate branch, a traditional offering for the dead.

FARMING IN GREEK AND ROMAN TIMES

Most people in ancient Greece and Italy lived by farming, so Demeter (Ceres to the Romans) was a very important goddess for them. Greek and early Roman farms were usually small, producing just enough food to feed a family. However, by the time of the Roman Empire, some rich landowners ran huge farms that exported wheat all over the empire.

In ancient Greece and Italy, the main crops were wheat and barley, which were used to make bread and porridge. Most farmers also grew olives and grapes, which were crushed to make oil and wine. Pigs and poultry were kept for their meat, and sheep and goats provided milk and cheese. Mules and oxen were used as working animals to pull plows.

Persephone was delighted to be returning to the earth and her mother. But as she prepared to leave the gloomy underworld she had a brief moment of regret. She had learned to love her solemn husband and she was sad to be leaving Hades alone among the dead.

Hermes and Persephone traveled fast, but before they could reach the earth a messenger arrived with an urgent message from Hades. A worker in the garden of the dead had once spotted Persephone picking a pomegranate. She had eaten only seven tiny seeds, but that was enough. Now she could never leave Hades' kingdom. Persephone turned slowly back to join her husband, while Hermes flew to Mount Olympus.

When Demeter heard what had happened, she made a chilling announcement. Unless her daughter was released immediately, she would never care for the earth again. Zeus realized this would mean the end of humankind, so he wracked his brains for a solution. Eventually, Zeus came up with a possible plan, which he presented to his brother Hades. Could Hades agree to part with his wife for nine months each year, while she visited her mother on earth? Then, for the remaining three months of the year, Persephone could reign in the underworld with him.

PERSEPHONE'S RETURN

Hades was deeply saddened by this plan. However, he truly loved his wife and wanted her to be happy so, at last, he agreed. Filled with joy, Demeter made all the plants flourish and the weather grow warm again—all in honor of her daughter's return. During the months that Persephone stayed on the earth, the plants continued to grow and the weather was fine, but as soon as she left for Hades, Demeter neglected the earth again. Only when it was time for her daughter to return did Demeter start to care for the plants once more.

So, a pattern began that has continued ever since. For nine months of the year, in spring, summer, and fall, crops and plants flourish, but in the three winter months all the crops die. Then the farmers wait for Persephone, the spirit of the spring, to return to the earth once more.

Opposite: This Roman mosaic shows a farmer picking olives. Olive oil had many uses in ancient Greece and Rome. It was used in cooking and burned in oil lamps, but was also a major ingredient of cosmetics and medicines.

Greek and Roman Art

The artists of Greece and Rome established an elegant, naturalistic style that has been copied by artists ever since. The ancient Greeks were famous for their graceful sculptures and their striking vase paintings. Later, the Romans continued the Greek tradition of sculpture, and further developed the arts of mural painting and mosaic.

GREEK SCULPTURE

The sculpture of ancient Greece can be divided into three main periods. In the Archaic Period (c. 800–500 B.C.E.), sculptors carved simple, formal figures that were influenced by Egyptian art. Sculptors of the Classical Period (c. 500–323 B.C.E.) perfected the art of showing the human body in a realistic manner. In the Hellenistic Period (c. 323–30 B.C.E.), sculptors tackled a wider range of subjects in an expressive, dramatic style.

Left: The Charioteer of Delphi was sculpted around 478 B.C.E. in the Greek Archaic style. His finely cut, regular features inspired many copies from Roman times onward.

GREEK POTTERY

The potters of Athens used a red-colored clay to create two styles of pottery. In black-figure ware, artists used a black pigment made from ashes to paint their designs onto the red pottery (see p. 59). In red-figure ware, pots were first painted black, and then the designs were cut into the surface (see p. 14). White paint was added to show fine details.

Right: This dynamic horse and jockey, sculpted around the mid-second century B.C.E. shows the vigorous, lively style of the Greek Hellenistic Period.

ROMAN MOSAICS

All over the Roman Empire, mosaic artists created striking and often complex designs for floors and walls. The designs ranged from simple geometric patterns to elaborate scenes from myths. The mosaics were created using thousands of tiny cubes of colored glass, stone, or tile, known as tesserae. Mosaic making was extremely labor-intensive and demanding work. Artists used a range of subtle shades to make their subjects look realistic.

Above: This Roman mosaic shows a pair of guinea fowl. Roman mosaicists tended to worked mainly in black and white, using color highlights to create dramatic effects.

Right: As well as depicting subjects from everyday life or from myth, Roman wall paintings often showed scenes of gardens and the countryside. This elegant mural from a house in Pompeii, in southern Italy, dates from around the first century C.E. and shows Flora, the goddess of spring.

ATHENA AND ARACHNE

The great god Zeus had many remarkable children, but his favorite was his tall, gray-eyed daughter, Athena. None of the gods and goddesses had as many talents as Athena. She was the goddess of wisdom and war; the patron of crafts, dance, and music; and the special protector of the city of Athens.

As well as being a powerful goddess, Athena was also a good friend to humans. She invented the arts of spinning, weaving, and pottery, and passed on all these skills to men and women. She showed human beings how to make wheels and axes, how to plow fields and make sails, and how to play trumpets and flutes.

But, in spite of all her many skills, Athena had one serious flaw. She could never bear to have any rivals. If anyone ever claimed to be better than she was, at anything, she would immediately fly into a jealous rage. No gods or mortals dared to challenge Athena—except for one foolish girl, called Arachne.

CHALLENGING ATHENA

Arachne lived in a small village in the region of Lydia, in present-day Turkey. Lydia was famous for its weavers, and the young Arachne began to learn the demanding skill of weaving as soon as she was old enough to hold a shuttle—the piece of wood weavers use to pass the thread when working on a loom. By the time Arachne was fifteen, she was the fastest weaver in the whole of the Greek world. But Arachne was not just immensely skilled at using a loom. She also had the ability to create marvelous scenes from her imagination.

Everyone who saw Arachne's work agreed that she was a remarkably talented girl. But she was very conceited. People had even heard her boast that she was better at her craft than the great inventor of weaving, Athena herself. Arachne's mother begged her to be careful, but her foolish daughter would not be stopped.

THE ART OF WEAVING

Greek women of all classes were expected to spin and weave their family's clothes, and this tradition continued into early Roman times. The wife of Emperor Augustus, Livia (58 B.C.E.–29 C.E.), took great pride in weaving all her husband's clothes. However, by the second century C.E., most Roman weaving was done in professional workshops.

All Greek homes had a wooden loom where the women of the house worked. Everyday cloth was usually white with a simple patterned border, but some skilled weavers produced intricate patterns using a range of colored woolen threads. The wool was colored with natural dyes, which were made from plants and minerals.

Left: Even though Athena had many peacetime roles, she was almost always depicted fully armed, in her role as goddess of war. According to some legends, this is the way she first emerged into the world, bursting from the head of her father Zeus.

"But it's true," Arachne boasted carelessly, "I really am a better weaver than Athena!"

One day, a mysterious old woman arrived in Lydia and asked to see Arachne. She was led to the girl, who proudly displayed her work. "I bet you've never seen a tapestry like this," said Arachne. "Even Athena couldn't create designs as fine as mine."

"Be careful what you say, my girl," the old woman warned. "You know that a mortal can never compare with a god." And then, to the amazement of the frightened weavers, she suddenly transformed herself into a gleaming goddess, dressed for battle. Everybody fell to the ground except for bold Arachne, who held her head up high.

Left: This fresco, by the Italian Paolo Veronese, presents a sixteenth-century artist's view of the legend of Arachne. Veronese depicts Arachne, dressed in finely woven robes, admiring the industry of a spider.

"You have dared to challenge a goddess," Athena boomed, "so now I challenge you. We will hold a contest right here in the village square. And then we will really see who is the better weaver!"

The great weaving contest began at sunrise. Two large looms were set up, and the contestants settled down to work. Their shuttles flew so fast they looked like a blur, and under their fingers two marvellous tapestries took shape.

Both of the tapestries were filled with magnificent patterns, colors, and shapes, and both of them depicted the legends of the gods. But while Arachne created a playful scene of the gods in love, Athena chose the sterner subject of the power of the gods. Eventually both designs were completed and the weavers sat back to rest. Poor Arachne was close to collapse, and her fingers were torn to shreds. Athena looked calm and fresh, and her hands were as soft and white as when she had begun.

A JUDGMENT AND A PUNISHMENT

Athena ordered that the two tapestries should be hung together, so that their designs could be compared. The weavers stood back and surveyed their work. At first, neither of them spoke, but after a while Arachne began to smile. "My work is finer," the girl blurted out. "I really am a better weaver than Athena!" Everyone in the crowd gasped, but secretly they agreed.

Athena's face turned as black as thunder. The mighty goddess raised her sword to kill her boastful rival, but as she did so Arachne's mother dropped to her knees.

"Please pardon my daughter," she begged. "She's still only a child!"

For a moment, Athena's sword wavered, but then the goddess lowered it again. She was still furious with Arachne, but she could not help admiring her skill. Athena thought for a moment for a suitable punishment, and then she searched in her cloak for a handful of herbs. She sprinkled them over Arachne's head and stood back to watch.

The moment the herbs touched her skin, Arachne started to shrink. Her body grew small and hairy, and she started to sprout long limbs on every side. Eventually she shrank to the size of a coin, and scuttled away to hide in a corner in shame. Proud Arachne had become a humble spider!

Ever since that day, Arachne has remained a spider. She still weaves her beautiful designs, but now people run away when they see her coming, and nobody ever praises her work any more.

Daedalus and Icarus

Daedalus (ded-al-us) of Athens was a man of many talents. He was a brilliant sculptor, an architect, and an engineer. He was also a skillful carpenter. Most remarkable of all, he was a great inventor, who could find a solution to any problem. But having many talents can sometimes make you vain, and Daedalus began to believe that he was even cleverer than the gods.

Daedalus was given the task of teaching his nephew the craft of carpentry. The boy, whose name was Perdix, learned very fast, and some people judged that he was a better carpenter than his uncle. This made Daedalus furious. One day he took the boy to the top of a tower, promising to show him the wonders of Athens. While Perdix was gazing out to sea, Daedalus pushed his nephew off the top of the tower.

Daedalus was punished for his terrible crime by being banished from the city of Athens. So he set sail for the island of Crete, taking his young son, Icarus, with him. When he reached the island he was warmly welcomed by King Minos, who invited the great inventor and his son to live with him in his palace. Daedalus created many wonders for the king. He built magnificent baths and fountains, thrones, statues, and temples, but his greatest achievement was to create an underground maze for a savage beast known as the Minotaur (see pp. 66–69).

A DARING INVENTION

After many years on Crete, Daedalus grew homesick for his native city. He longed to see Athens again and to show his son the wonderful sights of the city. But Daedalus knew the journey home would not be easy. King Minos was determined that he should never leave Crete. Daedalus had to think of a secret way to escape from the island. He puzzled long and hard about this problem, and as he thought he watched the seagulls soaring overhead.

Classical Myth

"If only I could fly like those seagulls," Daedalus said to himself. And then he had a daring idea. He and Icarus would fly across the ocean!

Daedalus immediately set about creating his latest invention. He collected all the feathers he could find and sorted them according to size. Then he arranged the feathers in the shape of wings, and carefully stuck them together with wax. After several tries, Daedalus had a set of wings ready to strap onto his body. When he was sure that he was alone, he climbed a deserted hill and tied on his wings. He ran as fast as he could off the top of the hill, flapped his wings hard, and discovered he could fly. Daedalus was proud and delighted.

"Only a brilliant inventor could make wings like these," he said, as he fashioned a second pair for his son.

Right: This famous work by the eighteenth-century Venetian sculptor Antonio Canova shows Daedalus preparing to bind a wing onto his son's right arm.

39

Above: The story of Daedalus and Icarus has been a popular subject among artists for millennia. The Italian artist Carlo Saraceni (c. 1570–1620) painted this scene called *The Fall of Icarus* on a copper panel in 1606–1607. The story's tragic message is still relevant today: humans should beware of growing too conceited and flying too high.

On the morning Daedalus and Icarus planned to leave, the sky was clear and cloudless, and the sun was high. They carried their wings to a rocky cliff and strapped them on tightly. Icarus was anxious to be off, but first his father had some important advice for him.

"Fly right behind me," he told his son, "and do exactly what I do. Don't fly too low, or your wings will be weighed down by the spray from the sea. And don't go too high, or the heat of the sun will melt the wax that keeps the feathers in place. Just follow a steady course and keep close to me."

Daedalus launched himself off the cliff and began to fly straight toward Athens. As he flew above the sparkling waves, Daedalus congratulated himself. Once he reached the city, he thought to himself, his old crime would quickly be forgiven. When the people of Athens saw how clever he was, he would be welcomed with open arms!

FLYING HIGH

At first, Icarus flew straight behind his father, but flying was so much fun that he soon grew reckless. He began to swoop and soar just like the seagulls all around him. First, he dipped right down until his wings touched the waves, then he rose up higher and higher until he felt like a god far above the earth. Only when he felt the sun burning his back did he remember his father's words of warning—but it was much too late. The sun had already melted the wax on his wings. Faster and faster, Icarus hurtled toward the sea. He plunged into the waves and was drowned.

Meanwhile, Daedalus had almost reached the city of Athens. But when he turned to show the city to his son, Icarus was nowhere to be seen. Daedalus flew straight back across the sea, desperately searching for his boy, but all that he discovered was a pair of wings floating on the waves.

After his terrible loss, Daedalus continued to work as an inventor, but he never stopped missing his beloved son. Nor did he ever forget the lesson he had learned: that mortals should never aim to be as clever as the gods.

ARCHIMEDES

Archimedes (c. 287–212 B.C.E.) was a mathematician, astronomer, engineer, and the greatest inventor of the ancient world. He invented the pulley system for lifting loads, and the Archimedes screw, which could raise water to higher levels. He also used levers to lift heavy loads. Archimedes is believed to have said, "Give me a place to stand and a lever and I will move the entire world."

CHILDHOOD AND EDUCATION

The family was central to the Greek and Roman way of life. Babies were well cared for, and most children grew up within a caring home. Greek children usually lived with just their own parents, but Roman families were often much larger, including grandparents, cousins, uncles, and aunts. The sons of wealthy families went to school, while most girls and poorer boys learned the skills they would need for their adult lives at home.

LEARNING AT HOME

In both ancient Greece and Rome, children from poorer families did not go to school. Instead, they stayed at home and helped their parents in their work. A son might learn to help around the farm, or join his father in the family workshop, making pots or tools. Girls of all classes were taught by their mothers how to run a home. In ancient Greece, this included learning how to spin and weave cloth.

Above: Women in ancient Greece usually stayed at home and devoted themselves to caring for their children. This vase painting, dating from the sixth century B.C.E, shows a mother with her twins.

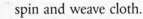

Left: Greek and Roman children might have a range of simple toys. Younger children played with rattles, dolls, balls, and spinning tops. Roman boys and girls played games of marbles and dice (as shown here).

SCHOOL TIME

Greek schools had three levels. At the first school, boys were taught basic reading, writing, and arithmetic. Then they moved on to a second school, where they learned poetry by heart and were taught to play the lyre. At a third school, they practiced athletics. Young men wishing to study further usually found a teacher to guide them.

Roman boys could attend two schools: a primary school, or *ludus*, and a secondary school, or *grammaticus*. Sometimes, wealthy girls were allowed to attend a *ludus*, until they were about eleven years old. There, pupils learned the basics of reading and writing. In the *grammaticus*, boys studied Greek and Roman literature, mathematics, history, geography, music, and astronomy. They also practiced the art of public speaking and trained in athletics.

Above: Some wealthy Greek and Roman boys—and even some girls—were educated at home by a tutor. This Roman painting shows a young girl with her writing equipment: a wax tablet, held in a wooden case, and a metal stylus, used for writing on wax.

Left: Carvings survive from Roman times showing children riding in miniature chariots, pulled by horses, goats, or geese. This carving is on a child's sarcophagus and dates from 150–160 C.E.

ECHO AND NARCISSUS

In the times of the gods, all the earth's mountains, fields, and forests were filled with nymphs—spirits of the countryside who took the form of beautiful young girls. These nymphs wandered happily through the land, swimming in the streams and playing in the meadows. The mountain nymphs were special favorites of the great god Zeus, who loved to while away the hours with them.

Zeus's wife, the goddess Hera, did not approve of Zeus's idea of fun. Whenever her mighty husband went sneaking down to earth to play with the nymphs, Hera came chasing after him, ready to lead him straight back to Mount Olympus. So Zeus dreamed up a cunning plan.

Of all the nymphs of the mountains, Echo was the friendliest. She loved to gossip and chatter with her companions. In fact, Echo was so good at talking that nobody could stop her. Zeus saw how he could use this to his advantage.

The next time Zeus descended to Earth, he arranged for Echo to intercept the jealous Hera and keep the goddess chatting. Hera spent a long afternoon listening to Echo's many stories, giving Zeus plenty of time to frolic with her companions.

ECHO'S PUNISHMENT

But goddesses are hard to deceive, and Hera soon discovered Zeus's trick. She was furious with the chattering nymph and decided to give her a suitable punishment. Hera pronounced that Echo would never speak a proper sentence again. Instead she would only ever be able to repeat the last few words of anything anyone said to her.

Poor, talkative Echo was distraught. Nobody wanted to hear their own words echoed back to them, so all her friends kept well away from her. Echo became pale and thin and took to hanging around caves and rocks, looking on wistfully while others were having fun.

BEAUTY CARE

Looking good was very important to the ancient Greeks and Romans. Men and women bathed every day and rubbed their skin with perfumed oils. Roman women smoothed powdered chalk onto their faces and arms to make them fashionably pale. They colored their cheeks red with pigment and darkened their eyebrows with soot. Some ladies tried to stay looking young by using a face cream made from crushed-up snails.

As today, fashions in hairstyles came and went. In the Classical Period in ancient Greece, women of all classes tied up their hair with ribbons, scarves, or nets. In the second century C.E., wealthy Roman ladies had incredibly elaborate hairstyles, with curled and braided hair held in place by dozens of pins. Some Roman women also wore wigs and hairpieces, which were usually made from the hair of slaves.

Left: Roman women kept pots of makeup and perfumes in cases such as this decorated first-century C.E. box. It contains a metal plate for mixing powders and ointments.

Above: This Roman fresco, from the first century B.C.E., shows the beauty routine of a wealthy lady. A maid helps the woman to style her hair, while a slave boy holds up a mirror of polished metal.

FOLLOWING NARCISSUS

One day, Echo was wandering through the forest when she saw the most beautiful boy she could ever have imagined. He was called Narcissus and he had wonderful thick curly hair and sparkling eyes. Echo fell madly in love with him and started to trail behind him silently. This did not please Narcissus at all. He was a very vain young man, whose mother had constantly told him that no girl could possibly be good enough for him. To make matters worse, whenever Narcissus tried to speak to Echo, she simply repeated his own words back to him. In the end, the cruel boy took to taunting the wretched Echo.

"Go away and don't come back!" he would shout.

"Come back!" mournful Echo replied.

"I will never love you!"

"Love you!" she called.

But however cruelly Narcissus treated her, Echo could not stop loving him and she still followed him wherever he went.

All the time that Echo had been suffering, the goddess Artemis had been watching over her. Artemis was sorry when Hera punished Echo, but she knew that she could never defy the queen of the gods. However, when she saw Narcissus teasing Echo, Artemis decided it was time for action. She would teach vain Narcissus a lesson that he would never forget.

THE VISION IN THE POOL

The next time Narcissus was riding through the forest, he was suddenly seized by a terrible thirst. He stopped at a pool to drink, and as he bent his head toward the water he saw a sight that made him gasp. Just beneath the surface of the pool a beautiful creature was staring up at him.

Narcissus fell instantly in love with the watery spirit. Eagerly, he plunged his arms into the water so that he could hold the creature in his arms, but straight away the spirit shattered into pieces. Narcissus pulled back in surprise, and gradually the spirit returned to the surface once more. Slowly, the terrible truth dawned on Narcissus: the creature that he loved so desperately was a reflection of himself.

Now, at last, Narcissus knew how it felt to love somebody hopelessly, just as Echo loved him. Day after day, he lay by the pool, unable to wrench himself away, while Echo stood by mournfully, powerless to help. Slowly the two wretched souls grew weaker and weaker until they finally wasted away. All that was left of Narcissus was a

Above: In 1903, the English artist John Waterhouse painted his impression of the legend of Narcissus. The beautiful youth gazes adoringly at his own reflection, while golden narcissus flowers grow around the edges of the pool.

golden flower growing beside the pool, while Echo shrank to a plaintive voice that could frequently be heard up in the mountains.

The gods had punished Echo and Narcissus cruelly, and they were both condemned to suffer forever. Even today, the golden narcissus flower still grows beside water pools, turning its beautiful face toward its own reflection. The voice of Echo still lives among the mountains, sending back its sad and ghostly replies.

The adventures of the ancient heroes take place partly
in a mythical landscape and partly in the real
Mediterranean region, as the heroes climb high
mountains; shelter in caves; and sail past rocky cliffs,
such as those of the Italian island of Lipari, seen here.

ANCIENT HEROES

Many of the best-known classical legends tell the stories of heroes. The superheroes of the ancient world—Heracles, Odysseus (oh-DIS-ee-uhs), Perseus, and Theseus—all set out on amazing journeys and do battle with terrifying monsters. They suffer intense hardships and endure agonizing setbacks. Sometimes they are tricked by enemies, and sometimes they are punished because of their own weaknesses. But they are always tested to their limits. At the end of the stories, the heroes have proved that they can overcome any challenge, as long as they are armed with virtue, courage, and determination.

The myths of the ancient heroes demonstrate, in larger-than-life terms, how people have to face whatever challenges life throws at them. They also show how even superheroes have to overcome character flaws. But these ancient stories are much more than just teaching tools. With their constant thrills and spills, they are also fantastic entertainment. It is no wonder that the legends have been told again and again—in poems, plays, paintings, and movies.

THE ADVENTURES OF PERSEUS

The story of Perseus began in the kingdom of Argos, where Acrisius (ak-RIS-ee-us) was the king. Acrisius was a coward who had one terrible fear: he had once been told that he would be killed by a child born to his daughter, Danae. Little did he realize that his grandson would be the famous hero Perseus.

King Acrisius was so frightened by the prophecy that he kept his only daughter locked away in a bronze tower so that she could bear no children. The unhappy Danae had to spend her days in a windowless prison. But the king was powerless to protect his daughter from the immortals, and one night Zeus entered the tower in a beam of light. Very soon afterward, Danae bore a son, whom she called Perseus. When Acrisius saw the child, he turned white with fear. Here was the grandson he had always dreaded!

Acrisius gave orders that the mother and child should be banished from his kingdom. Danae and her baby were thrown into a wooden chest and launched onto the waves to meet a watery death. For days the chest was tossed on the ocean, but at last it was washed up on the shore of the island of Seriphos, in the Aegean Sea. There, it was found by a fisherman called Dictys, who took the exhausted mother and child home to live with him.

Perseus spent a happy childhood on Seriphos, and he grew up to be strong, handsome, and wise. Everybody loved him, except for Polydectes (poly-DECK-tees), the island's ruler. King Polydectes was a cunning and conceited man who was determined to make Danae his bride, but Perseus protected his mother fiercely.

POLYDECTES'S CHALLENGE

By the time Perseus was sixteen years old, Polydectes was desperate to be rid of him. So the king laid a trap for him. He announced that he was holding a party and asked all his

Below: The gruesome head of Medusa was a popular subject for classical artists. Here she forms the centerpiece of a mosaic floor from second-century C.E. Roman North Africa. Medusa is also often known as the Gorgon.

Above: This Greek red-figure plate shows Danae with the baby Perseus landing on the island of Seriphos. They are welcomed by the fisherman Dictys.

guests to bring a special gift. Perseus was invited as well, even though he was much too poor to afford a present. On the day of the party, Perseus arrived empty-handed.

"Have you nothing to offer your king?" Polydectes mocked.

This angered Perseus, and he answered boldly, "Ask for anything you wish, and I will bring it to you."

Polydectes smiled to himself. Perseus had fallen straight into his trap. The king made a dramatic announcement: "Bring me the head of Medusa. That is the gift I want!"

All the guests fell silent when they heard the king's terrifying challenge. Medusa was a fearsome monster with writhing snakes for hair, and anyone who looked at her was instantly turned to stone.

But Perseus did not hesitate to reply. "I am a man of my word," he answered clearly. "I will find your gift and bring it back to you!"

GIFTS OF THE GODS

Before he left Seriphos, Perseus prayed to Athena for guidance, and, much to his amazement, she answered his prayers. The goddess appeared before him, holding out a shining shield.

"This is for you," she said, smiling. "Use it wisely when you find Medusa, and it will keep you safe."

Then Hermes swooped down to earth and presented Perseus with a pair of golden sandals. "These will help you fly across the earth," he said. Perseus strapped on the sandals straight away and started to practice his flying. But Athena had more advice to give.

"Before you meet Medusa, you will need three extra gifts: the helmet of invisibility, a magic pouch, and a strong, curved sword. These powerful gifts all belong to Hades, king of the underworld. They are kept by the three Stygian maidens, who live on the banks of the Styx River, and you must travel down to the underworld to find them."

MEETING MEDUSA

Perseus thanked Athena with all his heart, and flew off to find the Styx River. The journey took several months and was full of dangers, but he finally reached the gloomy banks of the river. There he found the Stygian maidens waiting for him, ready to present their precious gifts.

Armed with his gifts, Perseus flew directly to Medusa's fearsome cave, which was far away across the oceans. As he approached the entrance to the lair, he noticed that all the boulders had human shapes—these were the victims that Medusa had turned to stone! He could hear the hissing of a hundred poisonous snakes. Perseus stopped and thought hard about Athena's advice. How could a shining shield ever protect him against such a monster? Suddenly, he smiled to himself, put on his helmet of invisibility, and crept into Medusa's den unseen.

THE UNDERWORLD

The ancient Greeks and Romans believed that the souls of the dead went to dwell in the underworld, the gloomy kingdom below ground ruled by Hades. To reach the underworld, the souls had to travel by water until they reached the Styx, the river that divided the living from the dead. Charon the ferryman carried the dead on their journey, and Cerberus (ser-ber-us), a three-headed dog, guarded the banks of the Styx to make sure nobody ever returned from the land of the dead. Greeks and Romans were buried with a coin, called an *obol* (from the Greek for "metal rod"), placed beneath the tongue. This was the fare to be paid to Charon for their safe passage to the underworld.

Above: The Acheron River flows through northwest Greece. Its name means "river of woe," and the ancient Greeks believed that it was a branch of the Styx River. People believed that souls could start their journey to Hades' kingdom from this sacred spot.

Gazing into his shield, Perseus used the reflection to sidle close to the fearsome monster without looking straight at her. As he came within striking distance, Medusa heard his footsteps and reared up in anger, with her eyes flashing and all the serpents spitting around her head. She was a truly terrifying sight, but Perseus did not flinch. With his curved sword he took a mighty swipe at the monster, slicing her head clean off her body. The head gave a horrible groan and rolled heavily away into a corner of the cave. Mighty Medusa was no more.

Left: This sculpture, by the Italian artist Benvenuto Cellini (1500–1571), shows the victorious Perseus holding up the severed head of Medusa.

Above: Among his dramatic frescoes for the cathedral of Orvieto in Italy, Luca Signorelli (c. 1445–1523) painted Perseus freeing Andromeda. This version of the ancient legend shows Perseus as a medieval knight and Andromeda as a maiden in distress. Perseus fights a sea serpent that resembles a dragon, while Andromeda's parents look on in horror.

Perseus dropped Medusa's head into his magic pouch, without meeting its frozen stare, and set off for Greece. The journey home was long and hard, but he finally reached the coast of Africa, where he saw a terrible sight. A beautiful girl was chained to the rocks, while, at the top of the cliff, a man and woman were crying out in distress.

PERSEUS AND ANDROMEDA

Perseus landed on the cliff, and the desperate couple told him their story. They were King Cepheus and Queen Cassiopeia, and the girl in chains was their daughter Andromeda. Cassiopeia had foolishly boasted that her daughter was lovelier than Poseidon's sea nymphs, and now she was facing her punishment. The powerful sea god Poseidon had chained Andromeda to a cliff and sent a savage sea monster to devour her. Looking out to sea, Perseus could see the serpent racing toward them. He decided straight away to fight the monster and win Andromeda for himself.

As the serpent approached them, Perseus studied its massive scaly body and thrashing tail. It was a fearsome beast, but Perseus worked out a plan. He waited until the serpent was just inches away from Andromeda, and then swiftly dived for its head, plunging his sword down hard between the monster's eyes. The serpent twisted in agony, lashing out with its powerful tail. But Perseus had dealt it a deadly blow, and soon the sea was dark with its blood. Perseus unchained the weeping Andromeda, while her grateful parents gladly agreed to their wedding.

As soon as they were married, Perseus returned to the island of Seriphos with his new bride. There he was reunited with his mother Danae, who was overjoyed to see him again. But, before he could relax, Perseus had a promise to keep. He marched straight to the palace where King Polydectes was feasting with his friends.

"I have brought your gift," Perseus announced.

He pulled Medusa's head out of its pouch and held it up to his enemy, who immediately turned to stone.

A PROPHECY FULFILLED

Everyone on Seriphos was delighted to see the end of Polydectes, but Perseus did not stay to join in the rejoicing. He was eager to return to the land of his birth, so he sailed with Danae and Andromeda back to Argos. There, he found the young men of the region holding a sporting contest, and accepted their invitation to join in the games.

The main event of the day was throwing the discus, but this did not go according to plan. When Perseus threw the heavy disc, a powerful wind sent it spinning into the crowd. There it hit an old man, killing him stone dead. Perseus was horrified at what had happened. The old man was swiftly identified: he was none other than the cowardly King Acrisius. When he had learned that Perseus was in Argos, Acrisius had disguised himself and hid among the crowds. But there is no escape from the will of the gods. Perseus had fulfilled his destiny, and now he settled down to be a great and wise ruler.

DEMOCRACY AND POWER

The ancient Greeks and Romans tried several methods of governing their people, and some of these systems had a lasting legacy. The words they used to describe their forms of government—oligarchy, tyranny, democracy, republic, and empire—are still used today.

OLIGARCHIES, TYRANTS, AND DEMOCRACY

During most of the Greek period, people lived in city-states. These were small, independent kingdoms that were based around a city. The first such city-states were ruled by groups of aristocrats, in a system known as an oligarchy (which comes from the Greek for "rule by the few"). In some city-states, a single powerful man known as a tyrant (meaning "military leader") rose to take power alone.

In 508 B.C.E., an aristocrat called Cleisthenes came to power in Athens and introduced a radical new system of government, called democracy (from the Greek for "rule by the people"). He set up an assembly in which every citizen could speak and have a vote. The Athenian system was not a true democracy as we understand it today, because it excluded women, slaves, and people born outside the city. However, the idea of a government that consulted the people became an inspiration for later democracies.

Left: The Greek politician Pericles (500–429 B.C.E.) was a great supporter of democracy. He started an ambitious building program to improve the city of Athens, and introduced measures to make life easier for the poor.

REPUBLIC AND EMPIRE

For the first three centuries of its history, Rome was ruled by kings, but in 510 B.C.E., the Romans drove out their last king and established a republic (from the Latin for "public matter"). The Roman Republic was governed by a Senate, a group of 300 men from the most important families in Rome. Senators were appointed for life but they were expected to serve the Roman people and spend their money on public buildings and projects to help the poor.

The Senate was led by two consuls, who were elected by the free men of Rome every year. This system was supposed to stop any single man from becoming too powerful. But in times of trouble, the Senate appointed one very strong man to lead them, as dictator (from the Latin for "to assert"). In 45 B.C.E. Julius Caesar was declared dictator for life by the Roman Senate and started to rule without consulting anyone. He was soon assassinated by a group of senators, but in 27 B.C.E. his heir, Augustus, took complete control of the Roman lands. He is considered to be the first of a long line of Roman emperors. Although the Senate still existed, the emperor took all the important decisions about the way his empire was run.

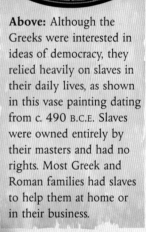

Above: Although the Greeks were interested in ideas of democracy, they relied heavily on slaves in their daily lives, as shown in this vase painting dating from c. 490 B.C.E. Slaves were owned entirely by their masters and had no rights. Most Greek and Roman families had slaves to help them at home or in their business.

Left: Some Roman emperors were self-indulgent and weak, but others worked hard at the job of ruling their people. Emperor Hadrian (117–138 C.E.) was an excellent military leader who traveled widely through the empire, giving orders for buildings to be constructed.

THE LABORS OF HERACLES

Heracles was the greatest of all the ancient heroes. His mother was Queen Alcmene of Thebes and his father was the great god Zeus. Yet he also had a powerful enemy. The goddess Hera was jealous of all Zeus's children, but she loathed Heracles most of all.

When Heracles was still a baby in his cradle, Hera sent two serpents to poison him. But the infant Heracles was already endowed with mighty strength and he managed to strangle the snakes with his bare hands. This made Hera even more determined to destroy him.

Despite the goddess's anger, Heracles grew up to be a remarkable young man. He was skilled at wrestling, fencing, and archery, and he was also noble and brave. His first great deed was to defend Thebes from the troops of the city of Orchomenus, which lay to the north. Heracles was rewarded for this feat with the hand in marriage of Megara, a princess of Thebes, and together they had many children. Heracles and Megara were happily married, but jealous Hera decided to put a stop to all that. She infected Heracles with a mindless rage which made him murder his wife and all his children.

When his rage had ebbed away, Heracles was devastated by what he had done. He went straight to Delphi, to visit the oracle, a wise priestess who spoke for the god Apollo. Heracles begged the oracle to find a suitable punishment for his crimes.

"Nothing would be too hard," he groaned, "to make amends for my terrible deeds."

Heracles waited patiently to hear his fate, and, at last, the oracle spoke. "Go to the city of Tiryns and offer yourself as a servant to King Eurystheus (you-ris-thee-us). He will be your taskmaster and you must carry out everything he asks you to do. If you perform all his tasks faithfully, Apollo will grant you forgiveness and you will find peace at last."

THE NEMEAN LION

As soon as Heracles reached Tiryns, King Eurystheus made his first request. For many years, the people of Nemea had been terrorized by a massive lion, and Heracles' first task was to kill and skin the savage creature.

Heracles climbed the hills until he reached the entrance of the lion's blood-spattered cave. He was prepared to fight the beast with all his finest weapons.

First, Heracles shot all his arrows at the lion, but they bounced off its flanks like a shower of rain. Then he thrust his sword into the creature's chest, but the lion simply roared and lunged back at him. Then he tried to batter it to death with his giant club.

When even this massive weapon did not work, Heracles decided that he would have to tackle the lion with his bare hands. He flung himself at the creature's throat and used his incredible strength to choke it to death. Then he used one of the lion's own razor-sharp claws to skin the beast.

ALEXANDER THE GREAT

Alexander the Great (356–323 B.C.E.) was a real-life Greek hero whose father, Philip II of Macedon, had unified the Greek city-states under his rule.

Alexander was often compared to Heracles by the Greeks. He was an outstanding military leader who conquered land all over the Middle East and became ruler of Egypt. Alexander inspired great loyalty in his men and led his army for thousands of miles, even reaching northern India. He died at the age of thirty-two, having won more land than any other man in the history of the world.

Left: Alexander the Great modeled himself on Heracles. Sculptors often show Alexander wearing a lion's skin, just like the legendary hero.

THE HYDRA

Heracles returned in triumph to King Eurystheus, dressed in the lion's skin. But the king did not bother to congratulate the hero. Instead, he set him his next task. Heracles had to kill the many-headed Hydra, a vicious water serpent whose body was filled with poison. Originally, the Hydra had nine snake-like heads, which all spat venom, but now it had too many heads to count. Whenever anyone dared to cut off one of its heads, it simply grew two more! Nobody had ever worked out how to defeat the monster, but Heracles had a plan.

While he battled the creature, Heracles made his servant Iolus stand beside him holding a flaming torch. Every time he lopped off one of the Hydra's heads, he quickly applied the torch to seal the wound. In this way, Heracles finally succeeded in destroying the poisonous monster.

A STAG AND A BOAR

When King Eurystheus heard about the Hydra's death, he was very angry. He claimed that Heracles had not obeyed his command, because he had used a helper in his task. The king had intended to set Heracles ten labors, but now he determined to make it eleven. He immediately set a new task. This time the hero had to find and capture the stag of the goddess Artemis. The stag was a noble creature with golden antlers and hooves of brass. It could run as fast as the wind, but the gods would never allow anyone to harm it.

Heracles chased the stag up and down mountains, until they were both exhausted. Eventually, the stag could stand the chase no more and it lay down in a meadow to rest. Heracles crept up silently behind the sleeping stag and carefully lifted it onto his back. Then he set off for the palace. Heracles was anxious not to offend the gods, so as soon as the king had seen the magical stag he released it back into the wild.

Heracles' fourth task was to capture a wild boar that lived in the mountains. It was a gigantic, bristling beast with tusks as long as a man's arm, and it terrorized the people for miles around. Heracles drove the boar higher and higher up a mountainside until it finally stumbled into a snowdrift. He bundled it into a net and carried it back to the king.

Below: After Heracles had killed the lion of Nemea, he often dressed for battle in a lion's skin. In this Greek vase painting he is shown defeating an enemy, while the goddess Athena stands behind him, ready to offer divine aid.

STINKING STABLES

For his fifth labor, Heracles was given a disgusting task. He had to clean the stables of King Augeas of Elis in one day. The stables had not been cleaned for years, they were knee-deep in dung, and their stench polluted the air for miles around.

When King Augeas heard of Heracles' task, he laughed out loud. "It would take a thousand barrow-loads to clear all the muck from out of my stables," he chuckled, "and you have to clean them in just one day!"

Heracles said nothing, but the next day he climbed the hill above the stables until he reached a river. He used all his strength to push several huge boulders into the river's path. Then he simply stood back and watched as the river flowed straight down the hill and through the stables. By the end of the day, the stables were sparkling clean.

BIRDS, A BULL, AND HORSES

Augeas was delighted with his sweet-smelling stables, but King Eurystheus was furious. Instead of performing the task on his own, Heracles had used the river to do his work.

Angrily, the king announced that Heracles would now have to perform twelve labors, and wasted no time in setting the next task. Heracles had to rid the land of a flock of vicious birds with beaks and claws of brass. Faced with this daunting task, Heracles prayed to Athena, who gave him a giant rattle. Heracles took the rattle to the shores of a lake where the birds were resting and shook it as hard as he could. All the birds flew into the sky, screeching in alarm, while Heracles picked up his bow and poisoned arrows. He shot at the panicking birds until they were all either dead or had flown away in fright.

Heracles' next task took him to the island of Crete, where King Minos was troubled by a wild bull. The bull had been given to Minos as a present by the sea god Poseidon, but now it was rampaging all over the island. Heracles swiftly tracked down the bull, caught it in his net, and returned with it to King Eurystheus. Then he set off for his eighth adventure in the land of Thrace.

Thrace was ruled by King Diomedes (die-OM-ed-ees), a cruel and violent man who had trained his horses to feed on human flesh. Heracles' task was to steal these horses and take them safely back to King Eurystheus. After many hours of chasing the beasts, he managed to round them all up, but then King Diomedes challenged him to a fight. After a long struggle, Heracles overcame the king and killed him.

The ravenous horses then feasted on their dead owner, but the moment they tasted the king's flesh they became completely tame. This made it an easy job to lead them back to the palace of Eurystheus.

THE MINOAN CIVILIZATION

King Minos of Crete features in many classical legends. This character was probably based on a real king, who ruled during the time of the Minoan civilization. The Minoans flourished on Crete from around 2000 to 1700 B.C.E. They built enormous palaces which contained hundreds of rooms. The ruins of the Palace of Knossos still survive on Crete today, and some historians believe that it was the home of the real King Minos.

Below: This fresco from the Cretan palace of Knossos dates from c. 1700 B.C.E. and shows the Minoan sport of bull leaping. The sport may have had a religious significance and was possibly linked to the legend of Heracles and the bull of Minos.

Above: In this Greek vase painting, Heracles is shown arriving at the palace of King Eurystheus with Cerberus, the three-headed guard dog of the underworld. The cowardly king is so frightened of Cerberus that he is hiding in a giant pot.

AMAZONS AND GIANTS

Heracles' ninth task was to win the girdle of Hippolyta, the queen of the Amazons. The Amazons were a race of powerful female warriors who lived on the shores of the Black Sea. Heracles arrived with a band of supporters prepared to fight for his life, but much to his surprise he was given a friendly welcome. Fierce Queen Hippolyta fell passionately in love with the hero and even promised to give him her girdle when he left. However, jealous Hera hated to see things going so well for Heracles, so she spread the rumor that he had come to carry off the queen. As soon as they heard this, a band of female warriors set off to save Hippolyta, but Heracles saw them coming. Suspecting a plot, he stabbed Hippolyta and seized her girdle. Then he set sail with his prize.

For his tenth labor, Heracles traveled to the western edge of the world. This was where the giant Geryon kept his herd of cattle. Geryon was a fearsome three-headed creature, and his cattle were guarded by a massive herdsman and a two-headed dog. Heracles had to battle with all three monsters to win the cattle, but this was only the beginning of his task. He still had to lead the cattle all the way back across the world. This exhausting journey took many months.

THREE APPLES

The next labor was to fetch three apples from the Garden of the Hesperides. No mortal could ever enter the garden and survive, but Heracles knew where he could find help. He hurried to the mountain where the giant Atlas lived. Atlas had been condemned by Zeus to hold up the heavens on his shoulders forever, and Heracles found the giant crouched on his mountaintop, burdened by the sky.

"Let me bear your load for a while," he said persuasively, "and in return you can do something for me." Atlas readily agreed to the plan and lumbered off happily to the nearby garden, while Heracles sweated and strained under the enormous weight of the sky.

When the giant returned, he tried a little cunning of his own. "Why should I give you the apples?" Atlas asked. "I could leave you here forever instead."

"If I'm going to hold up the sky forever, I will need to get comfortable," Heracles replied. "Just hold it for a moment, while I prepare to take the weight." So Atlas shouldered the sky once more, while Heracles grabbed the apples and raced down the mountainside as fast as he could.

THE FINAL LABOR

Heracles' twelfth labor took him to the shores of the underworld. His task was to collect Cerberus, the fierce three-headed dog who guarded the entrance to Hades' kingdom. It was a long and frightening journey, past all the spirits of the dead, but Heracles achieved this final task. After showing Cerberus to Eurystheus, the hero carried him back to Hades.

After this gloomy task, Heracles never visited the underworld again. As a reward for his labors, he was transformed into an immortal by the gods. His troubles were over at last, and he joined his father Zeus on Mount Olympus.

THESEUS AND THE MINOTAUR

From the moment he was born, Theseus was destined to be great. He was brought up by his mother, Aethra, who was queen of Troizen, in southern Greece, while his father was King Aegeus of Athens. Aegeus sailed for Athens before Theseus was born, but he left a special gift for his son.

Aegeus had hidden a magic sword beneath an enormous stone. He left instructions that, as soon as Theseus was strong enough to raise the stone on his own, he was to claim this gift and travel straight to Athens to join his father.

Theseus grew up to be brave and strong. Of all the boys in Troizen, he was the fastest runner, the strongest wrestler, and the best at hurling the javelin. Each day, Theseus grew a little stronger, until Aethra decided he was ready to claim his gift. She led him to the gigantic stone, which nobody could budge, and told him to try to lift it. Theseus pushed up with all his strength and, much to his surprise, it lifted easily. Theseus gazed in wonder at the precious sword his father had left for him.

Aethra urged her son to sail straight to Athens, but he insisted on taking the longer, overland route. Many giants and monsters lived in the wild lands between his homeland and the city of Athens, and Theseus was determined to overcome these tyrants and make the countryside safe to live in again.

The first person Theseus met on his journey was the fearsome giant Periphetes, who was armed with a heavy bronze club. Theseus had to dodge as fast as he could to avoid being battered to death. Eventually Theseus managed to stab Periphetes with his magic sword. He took the giant's club and continued until he reached the wood where Sinis, the pine-bender, lived. Sinis would stand between two trees and bend them until they touched the ground. He then tied passing travelers between the trunks, and let the trees spring apart, scattering their bodies in all directions. Theseus challenged Sinis to a fight and used the giant's club to defeat him. Then he made Sinis suffer the same terrible punishment that Sinis had given to his victims.

THE REVENGE OF KING MINOS

After defeating many more monsters, Theseus finally reached the royal palace at Athens. Aegeus was delighted to see his son, and together they reigned happily, but only until springtime came. At this time of the year the people of Athens were always seized with dread.

Years before, Aegeus had killed the son of King Minos of Crete, and ever since that time Minos had demanded his revenge. Every spring, fourteen young men and women were sent from Athens to the island of Crete. There they were sacrificed to the Minotaur, a terrifying monster with the body of a man and the head of a bull. The Minotaur lived in a labyrinth—a maze of passageways beneath the royal palace—and nobody ever emerged from that labyrinth alive.

Below: This mosaic, from a fourth-century C.E. Roman villa in Germany, shows Theseus fighting the Minotaur at the center of the labyrinth.

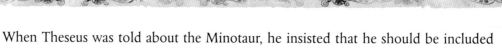

THE CITY OF ATHENS

Athens began as a small settlement on a hilltop, known as the Acropolis or "high city." Later, the city spread around the base of the hill, while the Acropolis was reserved for temples and shrines. By 500 B.C.E., Athens had become the leading city-state of the Greek world, and a thriving center for business, culture, and trade. At its peak, from around 479 to 431 B.C.E., the city attracted the best scholars, politicians, and artists of the Greek world.

When Theseus was told about the Minotaur, he insisted that he should be included among those to be sacrificed. He joined the group of thirteen young Athenians on the black-sailed ship leaving for Crete.

"I will try my best to defeat the Minotaur," Theseus told the crowd assembled at the harbor. "And if I am successful, this ship will have white sails when it journeys back to you."

When the Athenians reached the island of Crete, King Minos and his daughter, Ariadne, were waiting for them. As soon as Ariadne set eyes on Theseus, she fell in love with the handsome hero. She could not bear the thought that he would soon be sacrificed, and so she thought of a clever way to help him. When her father was looking the other way, she handed Theseus a large ball of wool.

"Use it carefully," Ariadne whispered, "and it will help you escape from the labyrinth alive."

FACING THE MINOTAUR

The next day, Theseus was led to the labyrinth. There he was left to follow the maze of passageways that led to the Minotaur. But Theseus had not forgotten Ariadne's gift. Before he set out, he fixed one end of his ball of wool to the doorpost at the entrance to the maze. Then, unwinding the wool as he went, he followed the labyrinth's endless twists and turns until at last he heard snuffling and snorting. The sounds grew louder and louder, until he was suddenly face to face with the Minotaur.

The monster charged toward Theseus with a deafening roar, wrestling him to the ground and goring him with its horns. Theseus writhed in agony, but he fought back bravely. First he stabbed the beast with his magic sword, then he managed to wrench off one of its razor-

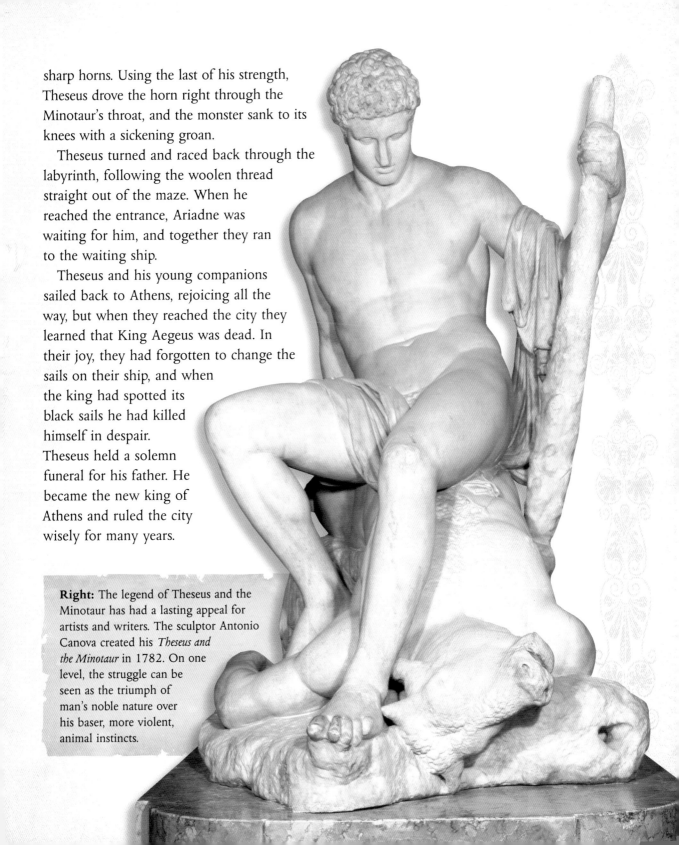

sharp horns. Using the last of his strength, Theseus drove the horn right through the Minotaur's throat, and the monster sank to its knees with a sickening groan.

Theseus turned and raced back through the labyrinth, following the woolen thread straight out of the maze. When he reached the entrance, Ariadne was waiting for him, and together they ran to the waiting ship.

Theseus and his young companions sailed back to Athens, rejoicing all the way, but when they reached the city they learned that King Aegeus was dead. In their joy, they had forgotten to change the sails on their ship, and when the king had spotted its black sails he had killed himself in despair. Theseus held a solemn funeral for his father. He became the new king of Athens and ruled the city wisely for many years.

Right: The legend of Theseus and the Minotaur has had a lasting appeal for artists and writers. The sculptor Antonio Canova created his *Theseus and the Minotaur* in 1782. On one level, the struggle can be seen as the triumph of man's noble nature over his baser, more violent, animal instincts.

Greek and Roman Architecture

The ancient Greeks developed a style of building that was balanced, simple, and elegant. Later, the Romans copied the Greek manner of building and added some new features of their own. Together the Greeks and Romans created a style of architecture that became known as "classical."

Left: Some smaller Greek buildings had carved figures, instead of columns, supporting their roofs. These figures are known as caryatids and they usually take the form of graceful maidens. This caryatid is holding up the porch of the Erechtheum, a temple in the Acropolis in Athens.

COLUMNS AND CARVINGS

Most Greek public buildings followed a very similar design. They were rectangular and had vertical columns supporting a sloping roof. The Greeks used two main styles of columns. Doric columns, as used in the Parthenon in Athens, were wide and sturdy, with undecorated tops (known as capitals). Ionic columns, in contrast, were slender, and their capitals were carved with twin stone curls. Most Greek buildings were decorated with carved and painted figures. A series of scenes ran in a frieze around the base of the roof, while the pediment (the triangular area at the front of the roof) was usually filled with tall, carved figures.

Opposite:
The Parthenon in Athens, constructed in the 440s B.C.E., was the largest of all the Greek temples, built to honor the goddess Athena. As the goddess never had a consort or lover, she was often known as Athena Parthenos, or "Athena the Virgin," from which the building takes its name.

Above: The Colosseum in Rome was completed in 80 C.E. Built as a stadium for public entertainments, it could hold a crowd of up to 50,000 people. The Colosseum was very cleverly designed, using arches and concrete to keep the weight of the upper structure to a minimum. Apart from the bottom level, which is built from solid marble, the other walls are made from a brick shell, which is filled with concrete and faced with marble.

ARCHES AND CONCRETE

The Romans continued to build in the Greek style, but they added the feature of the rounded arch, which was able to support a great deal of weight. They used several layers of arches, one above the other, to construct some very tall buildings. Roman builders also invented concrete, which was made by mixing volcanic ash with water, and adding small stones to give it extra strength. By filling the walls of their buildings with concrete, the Romans could build structures that were strong but also light. This meant that they could design much larger and taller buildings than ever before.

Left: Wealthy Romans often built themselves attractive country villas. These spacious, single-story homes had many airy rooms, linked by a series of courtyards and gardens. Inside the villa, walls might be decorated with frescoes and the floors with mosaics.

THE WANDERINGS OF ODYSSEUS

Odysseus was a hero of the Trojan War, and one of the bravest leaders of the Greeks. After ten long years of fighting, the Greeks managed to win the city of Troy, and it was finally time for them to return home. Odysseus set sail gladly for his kingdom of Ithaca, expecting to be home in just a few weeks. However, the gods had other plans for him.

Early in his voyage, Odysseus's ship was blown onto the shore of a small rocky island. All the crew were exhausted, so they could not believe their luck when they discovered a warm, dry cave that was lined with goats' skins. Even better, at the back of the cave there was a huge bowl of milk and some enormous cheeses. The men all enjoyed a hearty meal and lay down contentedly to sleep. But they had not been sleeping long when they felt the earth shake beneath them. Then they heard a rumbling voice and saw a massive pair of hairy feet. They had settled down for the night in a giant's cave!

The men watched in horror as the giant, whose name was Polyphemus, herded his flock of goats into the cave. Then they gasped in despair as he rolled a gigantic stone over the cave's mouth, trapping them all inside.

Left: The head of a hero: a Greek sculpture of Odysseus dating from the first century B.C.E.

The Greeks huddled at the back of the cave as Polyphemus sat down to eat. First he slurped up all the remaining milk and gobbled down the cheeses, then he grabbed some goats and swallowed them whole.

Only when he had finished eating did Polyphemus look around the cave. Then the crew had a chance to see just how frightening he was. The giant was a cyclops, with one single, glaring eye in the middle of his forehead.

It was not long before Polyphemus spotted the Greeks. "Who are you?" he boomed, "and what are you doing in my cave?"

"We are Greeks," Odysseus answered bravely, "and we seek shelter on your island."

THE TROJAN WAR

The dramatic events of the legendary Trojan War were described by the Greek poet Homer in the eighth century B.C.E. In his long poem called the *Iliad*, Homer tells how the Greeks laid siege to Troy, a city in Phrygia, in present-day Turkey. Some historians have suggested that the war that Homer describes may have been based on a real war fought around 1250 B.C.E. Homer also wrote a second poem, called the *Odyssey*, describing Odysseus's many adventures on his way home from the Trojan War. Odysseus's adventures were probably partly invented by Homer and partly based on ancient legends and stories.

Above: A story in the *Iliad* tells how Odysseus left the Trojans a gift of a giant wooden horse, like this modern reconstruction in Turkey. The Trojans took the horse inside their city walls, then a horde of Greek soldiers burst out of it and attacked the city.

The giant made no answer. Instead he lunged toward the men, grabbing two of them in his meaty fists. He stuffed his victims greedily into his mouth, rubbed his enormous belly, and settled down to sleep. Soon the cave was filled with deafening snores.

The crew urged their leader to kill the monster with no delay, but cunning Odysseus was too clever for that. "We would never be able to roll the stone away from the door, so if we kill him now, we will be trapped here forever. We must think of a better way to escape."

TRICKING POLYPHEMUS

All night, Odysseus thought about the problem, and by the morning he had come up with a solution. He waited patiently while Polyphemus led his goats out into the sunlight, and looked on calmly as the giant rolled the stone across the mouth of the cave. As soon as he heard the giant walking down the mountain, Odysseus gave his orders.

First, his men had to take one of the giant's massive walking sticks and sharpen its end to a point. Then they were to harden the point in the fire, and hide the stick under some straw. Finally, they each had to prepare some lengths of grass to use as ropes. After this, Odysseus explained his plan, and they all settled down to wait.

When evening came, Polyphemus returned to the cave with his flock. Once again, he ate an enormous meal, finishing off with a human snack, and then lay down to sleep.

As soon as Odysseus was sure that Polyphemus was sound asleep, he tiptoed up to the snoring giant and plunged his pointed stick as hard as he could into the cyclops' single eye. Polyphemus awoke with a deafening bellow of pain. He was in agony, but, even worse than that, he was completely blind! The giant blundered around his cave hitting out at the Greeks, but it was easy for them to keep out of his reach. Then Polyphemus sat and nursed his wounded head, thinking of a way to catch his tormentors.

The next morning, Polyphemus rolled the stone away from the cave door to let out his goats to graze. He was determined that none of the Greeks should escape, so he sat by the entrance feeling the back of each goat as it left the cave. However, cunning Odysseus had ordered his men to tie themselves to the bellies of the goats, so they could all leave the cave in complete safety. Once they were out of the cave, the crew hurried back to their ship and sailed away as fast as they could.

Right: This carved head of Polyphemus was made in Italy around 150 B.C.E. Polyphemus was one of the cyclopes, a race of one-eyed giants, who were all descended from the sons of Gaia, the goddess of the earth.

CIRCE THE ENCHANTRESS

After he had left Polyphemus safely behind, Odysseus had many more adventures, until he reached the island of Circe, the enchantress. As soon as they had landed, some men set out to explore, but only one of them returned. Shaking with fear, the man reported the terrible news. His companions had dined in Circe's palace, and they had all been transformed into a herd of snorting, snuffling pigs!

Odysseus set off straight away to rescue his men, but on his way to the palace he met a mysterious stranger. This was Hermes, the messenger of the gods. Hermes showed Odysseus where a white-flowered herb grew, and told him to pick some flowers to protect himself. When Odysseus arrived at Circe's palace, he had a bunch of magic herbs hidden in his cloak.

Circe welcomed Odysseus and gave him a wonderful feast, treating him as an honored guest, but as soon as the meal was over, she struck him on the shoulder with her wand. "Farewell, stranger," she hissed in his ear, "now you must go to the sty to join your fellow pigs!" Then she stood back, smiling, waiting for him to grow some trotters and a snout.

When Circe realized that Odysseus was unchanged, she grew very frightened. She knew that no one could withstand her magic, unless he was protected by the gods. She dropped to her knees and begged for mercy. Odysseus promised to spare her life on the condition that she turned the herd of pigs back into men. After doing so, Circe welcomed the Greeks as guests to her palace. She even tried to persuade Odysseus to stay forever, but his crew were anxious to head for home.

SIREN SONGS

Before Odysseus said farewell to Circe, she warned him about the sirens. They were enchanting young women who sang so sweetly that anyone who heard their song wanted to hear it forever. The rocky shores where the sirens lived were scattered with the bones of desperate sailors who had leaped from their ships to follow the heavenly music.

Right: A Greek red-figure vase shows Odysseus tied to the mast as he listens to the sirens' songs. In this imagining of the legend, the sirens take the shape of beautiful birds as they swoop about the ship.

Odysseus listened carefully to this warning, and ordered all his men to plug their ears with wax. However, he longed to hear the sirens' song, so he asked to be tied firmly to the mast. "However hard I struggle," he said, "do not let me go."

As the ship slipped past the coast of the deadly sirens, the crew kept on rowing, undeterred. But Odysseus was desperate to be free. He strained against his ropes with all his strength, so his crew had to bind him yet more firmly to the mast. The crew feared that the mast would break or their leader would go mad, but at last the singing began to fade away. When the sirens could be heard no more, Odysseus was released and the Greeks could continue on their long and eventful voyage back to Ithaca.

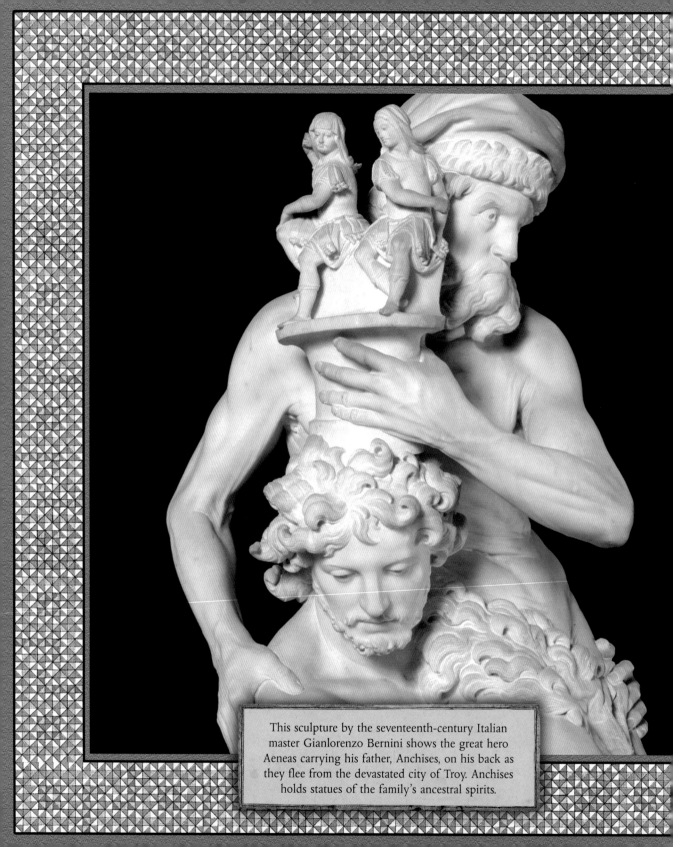

This sculpture by the seventeenth-century Italian
master Gianlorenzo Bernini shows the great hero
Aeneas carrying his father, Anchises, on his back as
they flee from the devastated city of Troy. Anchises
holds statues of the family's ancestral spirits.

ROMAN HEROES

During the second century B.C.E., the Romans gradually gained control of the Greek world. However, they did not destroy the culture of the Greeks. Many of the Greek gods and goddesses were absorbed into the Roman pantheon. There were few myths associated with the native Roman gods and goddesses, but the Romans adopted the Greek myths as their own. Roman writers, such as the poet Ovid (43 B.C.E.–17 C.E.), produced their own versions of the Greek legends. Roman artists depicted the ancient gods and heroes.

As well as retelling the Greek myths, the Romans also told some stories about their own early history. These legends were first told by the Latin people, who settled in central Italy around 1000 B.C.E. in a region later known as Latium. The two most important Roman legends were the founding of Rome by Romulus and the story of Aeneas. According to Latin legends, it was Aeneas who first brought their people to the region. The story was told by the poet Virgil (70–19 B.C.E.) in his poem the *Aeneid*. This famous poem tells the adventures of a great Roman hero but also incorporates many ancient Greek legends.

THE
ADVENTURES OF AENEAS

Brave Aeneas was one of the Trojan leaders in the famous Trojan War against the Greeks. He was the son of the goddess Venus, and his destiny was to found a new land, called Latium. After the Trojans' terrible defeat and the destruction of their city, Aeneas set sail with a fleet of ships in search of a new home for the survivors.

Aeneas had to face many challenges and dangers on his voyage before he could reach the land of Latium. After many months of traveling, the fleet reached Hesperia (present-day Italy), where they made landfall on the island of the harpies. Here Aeneas's men were attacked by screeching monsters with the heads of women and the bodies of hawks. Whenever the sailors tried to eat, the harpies swooped down and stole their food, so the exhausted Trojans were forced to sail away.

As the fleet passed the island of the Cyclopes, the Trojans were pelted with massive rocks thrown by the one-eyed giants, and, on the island of Sicily, they were showered with burning ash from Mount Etna. But perhaps the greatest challenge of all for Aeneas was to steer his ships through the narrow channel that lay between the grasping, six-headed monster of Scylla and the seething whirlpool of Charybdis.

Finally the Trojan ships arrived in calmer waters, and the travelers began to hope that they would soon reach their new land. But the goddess Juno had other ideas. She was determined that the son of Venus should never be allowed to fulfill his destiny, so she commanded Aeolus, the king of the winds, to use all his power to destroy Aeneas's ships.

For days the helpless Trojans were at the mercy of the winds, until powerful Neptune, god of the sea, took pity on Aeneas. Neptune brought the Trojan ships safely into port at the city of Carthage in North Africa.

DIDO OF CARTHAGE

Aeneas was relieved to feel solid ground beneath his feet again, but his troubles were far from over. Carthage was ruled by Queen Dido, a great favorite of Juno, and the goddess was determined that Carthage should become the greatest city in the world. So Juno sent Cupid, armed with his arrows of passion, to make Queen Dido fall in love with Aeneas. Juno's plan was for Dido to capture Aeneas with her charms, so he would never reach the land of Latium.

Aeneas was soon bewitched by Dido's beauty. For many months they lived together in her palace, until one day he had a visit from Mercury, the messenger of the gods.

GUARDIAN SPIRITS

In the opening scenes of the *Aeneid*, Virgil describes Aeneas's father, Anchises, carefully packing the statues of the family *lares*, the spirits of their ancestors, to take on their journey to the new land. The spirits of the ancestors were very important to the Romans, and all Roman homes had an altar for their lares. Whenever a family moved house, they always took their lares with them.

Right: This bronze Roman figure of a dancing lar dates from the first to third century C.E. Roman families prayed to their lares every day, and asked the spirits to keep their household safe.

"Have you forgotten your destiny, son of Venus?" Mercury asked sternly. "Why are you wasting your time on this foreign shore?"

As soon as he heard these words, Aeneas knew what he had to do. He gave orders for his ships to be prepared and steeled himself to face the furious queen.

"How can you betray our love and leave me all alone?" Dido screamed desperately.

But Aeneas knew his duty to the gods, and during the night he set sail secretly. By the time the sun rose, Aeneas was far away, searching once again for the land of Latium. Deserted, Dido killed herself in despair.

Below: The Frenchman Pierre-Narcisse Guérin painted Aeneas and Dido in c. 1815. Dido's passion for Aeneas was one of many challenges that the hero had to face on his travels.

ADVENTURES IN THE UNDERWORLD

After many more months of voyaging, Aeneas finally landed on the shores of Latium. He was delighted to have reached his destination, but he also longed to ask his father for advice. Wise old Anchises had died during the voyage and now Aeneas felt very alone. Perhaps, he thought to himself, he could make the journey down to the underworld and talk to Anchises one more time?

Aeneas asked a sibyl, a very wise woman, to guide him on his dangerous journey, and together they set off on the gloomy path that led to the underworld. On the way they passed all the shadowy troubles of human life—grief and disease, fear, hunger, and war—until they finally reached the Styx River, where Charon the ferryman was waiting to carry them to the kingdom of the dead. Once they reached the underworld, the sibyl led the way through the dark wood of the dead, past the gates of Tartarus, the pit of the damned, and out into the sunlit fields of Elysium. This was the heavenly home of the blessed, and there they found Anchises, waiting to welcome his son.

Aeneas was overjoyed to see his father again, and for a while they simply stood and gazed at each other in silence. But then Anchises led his son to a special place where the spirits of the future lived.

Above: Charon the ferryman prepares to carry the souls of the dead across the Styx River to the underworld. For most mortals, this was a one-way journey, but Aeneas presented a golden bough to Proserpine (Persephone), queen of the underworld, so that he could be allowed to return to earth.

"These are your descendants," he told Aeneas, showing him a long line of rulers, ending in a hero in a shining helmet. "And this last figure is Romulus, who will one day found the great city of Rome." Then the spirit of Romulus disappeared and his place was taken by a parade of warriors, kings, and leaders.

"Here are the future leaders of Rome," Anchises told his son. "There will be troubled times for the Romans, but there will be glory too, and one day Rome will rule the world." After this, father and son discussed the future of their people, until it was time for Aeneas to return to the land of the living once more.

THE ROMAN ARMY

In the early Roman period, there was no professional army. Only Roman landowners were called up to fight, and they had to provide all their own armor and weapons. However, around the year 100 B.C.E., a commander named Gaius Marius turned the Roman army into a full-time, professional fighting force. Marius allowed all Roman citizens to enlist, and provided armor, weapons, and training. He also organized the army into different groups of fighting men.

Left: A third-century C.E. carving shows Roman soldiers fighting Germanic warriors. The Romans wear helmets (shown below) and carry shields and swords, while the Germans are mainly unprotected.

ORGANIZING THE ARMY

The smallest unit in the imperial army was the *contubernium*. This was a group of eight men who fought closely together. Ten *contubernia* (eighty men) made up a century, which was commanded by a centurion. Six centuries (480 men) made up a cohort, and the largest unit was a legion, which was composed of ten cohorts. Altogether, the Roman army had a total of 25 to 35 legions, or 120,000 to 170,000 men.

Left: This second-century C.E. mosaic shows a group of Roman legionaries. In battle, soldiers wore a metal helmet and breastplate, while their legs and arms were protected by metal plates. Legionaries fought with a long sword and a dagger, and sometimes hurled javelins. They protected themselves with shields made from wood and metal.

Below: Julius Caesar (c. 100–44 B.C.E.) was a brilliant army commander. He conquered land in Turkey and in Gaul (present-day France and Germany), extending Roman territory as far as the English Channel. He produced seven books of detailed accounts of his military campaigns.

DIFFERENT ROLES

As well as soldiers, a legion included mounted messengers, engineers, and doctors. Most of the soldiers in the Roman army were foot soldiers, known as legionaries, but there were also some cavalry, who rode on horseback and could be very useful for rounding up groups of enemies.

Standard bearers carried the legion's emblem into battle, while *cornicenes* blew on large, curved horns to send signals to the troops. Many Roman armies also used foreign auxiliaries. These warriors from distant parts of the empire often had special skills, such as archery.

A SOLDIER'S LIFE

Life in the Roman army was very hard. As well as fighting in battles, soldiers were expected to march for up to 18 miles (29 km) a day, carrying all their equipment on their backs. Roman soldiers constructed their own forts and camps and, in peacetime, they built roads, bridges, and canals.

ROMULUS AND REMUS

For hundreds of years, the descendants of Aeneas ruled the beautiful city of Alba Longa, on the banks of the Tiber River. One of these rulers, King Silvius, was a wise and gentle man, and his older son, Numitor, was just like his father. But Silvius's younger son, Amulius, was cruel, ambitious, and selfish. When King Silvius died, he was succeeded by Numitor, but Amulius soon seized the throne from his brother, sending him to live in the countryside with his wife and children.

Amulius knew he had nothing to fear from gentle Numitor, but he was afraid that one day his brother's children would seize power from him. So he arranged for Numitor's two sons to be killed, leaving just his daughter, Rhea Silvia. When Numitor begged his brother to save the young girl's life, Amulius decided on a clever plan. He gave his niece a job as a vestal virgin. Vestal virgins were priestesses who served the goddess Vesta and lived in her temple. They were not allowed to marry, so Amulius could be sure that Rhea Silvia would never bear a son to challenge him.

THE BIRTH OF TWINS

Rhea Silvia settled down to life in the temple, but she was troubled by mysterious dreams. Seven times she dreamt that she was wearing a crown of leaves, with two tall trees sprouting up from it. The girl wondered if perhaps the dreams were a sign from the gods—and she was proved right. Very soon afterward, she gave birth to twin boys, the sons of the war god Mars, who had visited her while she was asleep.

When cruel King Amulius learned about the babies, he gave orders for Rhea Silvia and her sons to be drowned. The girl was dragged to the Tiber River and thrown into the swirling water. The two babies, screaming pitifully in their basket, were hurled into the river along with her. Then the king's servants returned to the palace to report that his orders had been obeyed. King Amulius was greatly relieved when he heard the news, and settled down to rule his subjects harshly. But no mortal could defy the will of the gods, and Mars did not stand idly by.

As his sons lay helpless in their basket, Mars made sure they were carried far from the city until they reached a tangle of roots by the riverbank. There, the basket lodged safely, and was discovered by a she-wolf, who lived in a nearby cave. Mars was the god of wolves as well as ruler of war, and he ordered the wolf to care for the babies as if they were her own. Instead of tearing the defenseless creatures to shreds, she gently picked up the boys in her mouth and carried them back to her den. She fed them with her milk, before they snuggled down to sleep beside her cubs.

Right: This famous Roman bronze statue has been copied many times. It shows the she-wolf suckling the twin boys, Romulus and Remus.

THE CITY OF ROME

Archaeologists believe that the city of Rome has its origins in the eighth century B.C.E., when a group of villages, built by the Latin people, merged into a town. Over the next 300 years, Rome grew into an impressive city with a central public square known as the forum, high defensive walls, and an efficient drainage system.

During the Roman period, the city went through many changes as powerful rulers added their own buildings, but the basic layout remained the same. At the heart of the city was the forum, containing the Senate house, the law courts, and temples to the gods. Surrounding these public buildings was a maze of streets lined by houses, shops, and apartment buildings.

Below: The ruins of the forum still stand at the heart of Rome. Three columns of the Temple of Castor and Pollux can be seen to the right, while the Temple of Vesta is in the center.

For a while the twins lived happily beside their wolf cub companions, but soon they were too old to survive only on the she-wolf's milk—and they needed different food from the hunks of meat the wolves devoured.

Ever watchful for his young sons, Mars ordered some birds to bring bread and fruit for the boys to eat. But it was not long before Faustulus, a local shepherd, began to notice the birds flying into the cave, and decided to investigate. When he saw the twins lying in the cave he snatched them up and raced back home.

"These are the children of gods, I'm sure," he told his wife, "and it is our duty to care for them."

Faustulus named the boys Romulus and Remus and brought them up to be honest, strong, and brave. By the time they were eighteen years old, the twins were expert farmers and hunters. They led a group of fearless youths who wandered freely over the fields and hills.

One day, the twins were roaming the countryside with their friends when Remus was captured and brought before a farmer as a trespasser. But, instead of blaming the boy, the farmer, whose name was Numitor, gave a sudden start of recognition. When Romulus arrived, looking for his brother, Numitor was certain of what he had suspected. He greeted his long-lost grandsons with tears of joy.

"The gods have granted me great happiness," he cried as he embraced them. He sat the twins down and told them all about their history.

FOUNDING ROME

When Romulus and Remus learned about their great-uncle's cruelty, they decided to take their revenge. Together they stormed the palace in Alba Longa and stabbed the wicked king.

The people were delighted when they learned that Amulius was dead. Numitor became king of Alba Longa, while Romulus and Remus—unwilling to live as mere subjects—decided to found a brand-new city on the slopes of the Palatine Hill, which is at the heart of Rome to this day.

But before they could even start work on building the city walls, the twins fell into an argument about the exact siting of the settlement. While Romulus began digging a trench where he thought the walls should run, Remus stood back and mocked his brother's work. Romulus flew into a rage, killing his twin outright. Romulus became king of the new city and, later, the city of Romulus was given the name "Rome."

CLASSICAL TIMELINE

c. 40,000 B.C.E.
The first people settle in Greece.

c. 4000 B.C.E.
A very early civilization develops on the Greek Cycladic islands, but soon dies out.

c. 1900 B.C.E.
The Minoan civilization rises on the island of Crete.

c. 1600 B.C.E.
The Mycenaean civilization rises in central Greece.

c. 1450 B.C.E.
The Minoan civilization declines, possibly wiped out by an earthquake.

c. 1150 B.C.E.
The Mycenaean civilization has collapsed.

c. 1100 B.C.E.
The so-called Dark Ages begin in Greece.

c. 1000 B.C.E.
The Latin people settle in central Italy.

c. 800 B.C.E.
The Archaic Period begins in Greece. The Greeks develop an alphabet.

776 B.C.E.
The first Olympic Games is traditionally said to be held at Olympia.

c. 750 B.C.E.
The city of Rome begins to grow. Greeks start to settle in lands around the Mediterranean Sea.

c. 600 B.C.E.
Etruscans from northern Italy sieze the city of Rome.

c. 510 B.C.E.
The last Etruscan king is driven out of Rome and the Roman Republic begins.

c. 508 B.C.E.
The democratic system is introduced in Athens.

c. 500 B.C.E.
The Classical Period begins in Greece.

338 B.C.E.
King Philip of Macedon becomes ruler of Greece. Rome takes control of all Latium.

336 B.C.E.
Alexander the Great becomes ruler of Macedonia and Greece.

332 B.C.E.
Alexander the Great conquers Egypt.

327 B.C.E.
Alexander the Great defeats Persia and advances to India.

323 B.C.E.
Alexander the Great dies and the Hellenistic Period begins in Greece.

312 B.C.E.
Work begins on the Appian Way, the first major Roman road.

c. 265 B.C.E.
The Romans have gained control of all of Italy.

197 B.C.E.
King Philip V of Macedonia is defeated by the Romans and gives up control of Greece.

146 B.C.E.
Rome controls all of Greece.

133 B.C.E.
Rome gains control of large areas of Asia.

107 B.C.E.
Gaius Marius reorganizes the Roman army.

88 B.C.E.
All Italians are given Roman citizenship.

73 B.C.E.
Spartacus leads a slave revolt in Italy.

63 B.C.E.
The Roman commander Pompey conquers four new provinces in the Middle East, including Judea.

58 B.C.E.
The Roman commander Julius Caesar begins a war to conquer all remaining parts of Gaul.

55 B.C.E.
Julius Caesar attempts unsuccessfully to invade Britain.

49 B.C.E.
Julius Caesar returns to Rome and seizes power.

44 B.C.E.
Julius Caesar is killed by a group of senators.

42 B.C.E.
Mark Antony and Octavian agree to divide the Roman world between them.

31 B.C.E.
Octavian defeats Antony at the Battle of Actium.

30 B.C.E.
Egypt becomes a Roman province.

27 B.C.E.
Octavian becomes the first Roman emperor, Augustus, as the Roman Empire begins.

43 C.E.
The Romans conquer Britain.

117 C.E.
The Roman Empire reaches its largest extent, under Emperor Trajan.

200 C.E.
Barbarians attack the Roman Empire's borders.

270 C.E.
Romans begin to abandon parts of the empire.

313 C.E.
Emperor Constantine allows Christians to worship freely.

395 C.E.
The Roman Empire splits into two parts: east and west.

455 C.E.
Barbarians invade Italy and attack Rome.

476 C.E.
Germanic tribes sack Rome, ending the Western Roman Empire. In the east, the Roman lands survive as the Byzantine Empire, ruled from Constantinople (Istanbul), for another 1,000 years.

GLOSSARY

archaeologist A person who studies human cultures of the past through analysis of architecture, artifacts, and other remains.

Archaic Period The early period of ancient Greek history, lasting from around 800 to 500 B.C.E.

barbarians The name the Romans gave to the people who lived outside the Roman Empire. The barbarians were mainly warlike warriors who worshipped their own gods.

black-figure vase A style of Greek pottery in which the design was painted onto the red surface of the clay using a black pigment made from ashes.

centurion An officer in the Roman army. They took their title from the fact that they commanded a hundred-man century, but centuries eventually changed to eighty men.

city-state An independent kingdom made up of a powerful city and the lands surrounding it.

classical A term used to describe the civilization, art, and culture created by the ancient Greeks and Romans.

Classical Period The middle period of ancient Greek history, lasting from around 500 to 323 B.C.E.

cyclops One of the race of giants with a single eye in the middle of their foreheads.

democracy A political system, introduced by the ancient Greeks, in which the citizens are consulted on how their state is run.

Elysium The heavenly place where the souls of the blessed go after death. Elysium is also known as the Elysian Fields.

frieze In architecture, a long band of sculpted or painted decoration.

Hellenistic Period The later period in ancient Greek history, lasting from 323 to 30 B.C.E.

innards The inner parts of a body, such as the heart, the liver, and the stomach.

labyrinth A maze.

lares Household spirits prayed to by Roman families.

Latins The Indo-European tribe who settled in the land of Latium and founded the city of Rome.

Latium The region of west-central Italy where the Latin people settled in around 1000 B.C.E.

legacy The impact made by a civilization, or a person, on the people who live after that civilization has ended.

legionary Roman foot soldier.

Minoans A race of people who established a very early civilization on the island of Crete. The Minoan civilization lasted from around 2000 to 1450 B.C.E.

Minotaur A monster with the body of a man and the head of a bull.

mosaic A decoration made from small pieces of colored glass, stone, or tile, which usually appears on a wall or floor.

Mount Olympus A mountain in central Greece. In classical myths, Mount Olympus was the home of the most important gods, known as the Olympians.

Mycenaeans A race of people who established a civilization in northern Greece. It lasted from around 1600 to 1100 B.C.E.

Olympians the most important gods, who lived with Zeus on Mount Olympus.

oracle A person believed to be able to foretell the future, often as the mouthpiece of the gods.

pantheon All the gods of a particular religion or mythology (from the Greek for "all gods").

red-figure vase A style of Greek pottery in which the pot was painted black and then had the design cut into the surface so it showed the red clay beneath.

Roman Empire 1. The vast area of lands controlled by the Romans. 2. The period in Roman history, lasting from 27 B.C.E. to 476 C.E., when the Romans controlled a vast expanse of land and were ruled by an emperor.

Roman Republic 1. The Roman system of government by a group of politicians called the Senate. 2. The period in Roman history, lasting from around 510 to 44 B.C.E., when the Romans were ruled by the Senate.

sarcophagus (plural **sarcophagi**) A stone container to hold a coffin or body. Sarcophagi were often carved or decorated.

sibyl A very wise woman who lived alone in a cave and had the ability to see the future.

stylus An implement used for writing on wax.

Styx River The river marking the border of the underworld.

Tartarus A deep pit in the underworld where wrongdoers were punished. Tartarus is also the name of the god ruling over the pit.

Titan One of a race of giants who fought a bitter war against the Olympians.

Trojan War A legendary war fought between the Greeks and the people of Troy, a city in present-day Turkey. The Trojan War may have been based on a real war fought around 1250 B.C.E.

tyrant A ruler with absolute, or total, power.

underworld The land of the dead. The underworld was ruled by Hades and is also known as Hades' kingdom, or simply Hades.

vase painting A general term for paintings on ancient Greek ceramic ware, including plates and bowls.

FOR MORE INFORMATION

BOOKS
The following is a selection of books that have been used in the making of this volume, plus recommendations for further reading.

Greek and Roman Myths
Buxton, Richard. *The Complete World of Greek Mythology*. New York: Thames & Hudson, 2004.

Daly, Kathleen. *Greek and Roman Mythology A-Z*. New York: Facts on File, 2003.

Gardner, Jane. *Roman Myths*. Austin: University of Texas Press, 1993.

Gibson, Michael. *Gods, Men and Monsters from the Greek Myths*. London: Peter Lowe, 1977.

Hamilton, Edith. *Mythology*. New York: Warner, 1999.

Houle, Michelle. *Gods and Goddesses in Greek Mythology*. Berkeley Heights: Enslow, 2001.

Morford, Mark and Robert Lenardon. *Classical Mythology* (7th edition). New York: Oxford University Press USA, 2006.

Usher, Kerry. *Heroes, Gods and Emperors from Roman Mythology*. London: Peter Lowe, 1983.

Greek and Roman Art and Culture
Beard, Mary and John Henderson. *Classical Art: From Greece to Rome* (Oxford History of Art). New York: Oxford University Press USA, 2001.

Bremmer, Jan. *Greek Religion*. Oxford: Oxford University Press, 2006.

Bingham, Jane, Reid, Struan, Chisholme, Jane et al. *The Usborne Encyclopedia of the Ancient World*. London: Usborne, 2003.

Haywood, John. *The Penguin Historical Atlas of Ancient Civilizations*. New York: Viking Penguin, 2005.

WEB SITES
www.perseus.tufts.edu
A massive searchable site of texts for all the Greek and Roman myths. This site also contains special illustrated features on Heracles and the ancient Olympics.

www.timelessmyths.com/classical
Simple retellings of all the major classical myths, with extra information on the cultural and historical background of the stories.

www.theoi.com
An illustrated guide to the gods, goddesses, monsters, and other creatures featured in classical mythology.

www.ancientgreece.co.uk
An interactive site on ancient Greece from the British Museum, London. The site includes opportunities to hear stories and undertake challenges.

www.roman-empire.net
A large site on the Roman Empire, divided into sections for different periods, with additional topic chapters on religion, society, and the army.

www.en.wikipedia.org/wiki/List_of_movies_based_on_Greco-Roman_mythology
A list of movies based on classical myths, organized by myth.

MUSEUMS
British Museum, London, UK
www.ancientgreece.co.uk
www.thebritishmuseum.ac.uk
The Department of Greek and Roman Antiquities contains over 100,000 objects dating from the third century B.C.E. to the fourth century C.E. The collections include the famous carvings from the Parthenon in Athens, and many fine examples of Greek and Roman jewelry, silver, and glass.

Metropolitan Museum of Art, New York, USA
www.metmuseum.org
North America's largest collection of classical art and sculpture. Objects range from small engraved gemstones to larger-than-life statues. The museum web site presents fifty highlights from the collections of Greek and Roman art.

National Archaeological Museum of Athens, Athens, Greece
www.culture.gr
The most important archaeological museum in Greece, covering all the cultures that flourished in ancient Greece, including the Minoan and Mycenaean civilizations.

The National Archaeological Museum of Naples, Italy
sights.seindal.dk/sight/1073_National_Archaeological_Museum
An astonishing collection of objects rescued from the excavated Roman towns of Pompeii and Herculaneum, which were buried in a volcanic eruption in 79 C.E. The web site shows over 300 exhibits from the museum's collection.

The J. Paul Getty Museum at the Getty Villa, Malibu, USA
www.getty.edu/museum
A modern reconstruction of a Roman villa, housing over 1,000 works of art from ancient Greece and Rome. The museum web site includes some virtual exhibitions of classical art, including sections on Roman mosaics and childhood in ancient Greece and Rome.

INDEX

ACKNOWLEDGMENTS

Sources: AKG = akg-images   **Scala** = Scala, Florence

b = bottom c = center t = top l = left r = right

Front cover: Corbis
Back cover: top akg-images, London; **bottom** Corbis

Pages: 1 Werner Forman Archive; **2–3** background: AKG/Erich Lessing; **3c** Scala/Museo Pio-Clementino, Vatican City; **7** Corbis/Yann Arthus Betrand; **8** Scala/Vatican Museum; **10** Scala/HIP; **13** Bridgeman Art Library/Louvre, Paris; **14** AKG/Erich Lessing/Musée du Louvre, Paris; **15** Bridgeman Art Library/Prado, Madrid; **16–17** Scala/Archaeological Museum, Delphi; **18t** Scala/Museo Nazionale, Naples; **18b** Scala/Bardo Museum, Tunis; **19br** AKG/Nimatallah/Museo Nazionale Archeologico; **21** AKG/Museo del Prado, Madrid; **23** Scala/National Archaeological Museum, Athens; **24** Bridgeman Art Library/Private Collection; **26** Corbis/Yannis Behrakis/Reuters; **29** Scala/National Museum, Reggio, Calabria; Scala/Bardo Museum, Tunis; **32t** Art Archive/Dagli Orti/Archaeological Museum, Delphi; **32b–33** Art Archive/National Archaeological Museum, Athens/Dagli Orti; **33t** Scala/Museo Nazionale Romano, Rome; **33br & 35** Scala/Museo Nazionale, Naples; **36** Scala/Doge's Palace, Venice; **39** AKG/Cameraphoto/Museo Civico Correr, Venice; **40** Scala/Museo di Capodimonte, Naples; **42t** Art Archive/Dagli Orti/Archaeological Museum, Tarquinia; **42b & 43t** Scala/Museo Nazionale, Naples; **43b** AKG/Erich Lessing; **45l** AKG/Tristan Lafranchis; **45br** AKG/Museo Nazionale Archeologico, Naples/Erich Lessing; **47** Bridgeman Art Library/Walker Art Gallery, National Museums, Liverpool; **48** Corbis/Jeremy Horner; **51tl** Scala/Museo Archeologico, Ferrara; **51cr** AKG/Gilles Mermet/Archaeological Museum, Tunisia; **52-53** Scala/Loggia dei Lanzi, Florence; **53** AKG/Erich Lessing **54** Scala/Orvieto Cathedral, Italy; **56** AKG/John Hios; **57t** Scala/HIP; **57b** AKG/Erich Lessing/Israel Museum, Jerusalem; **59** AKG/Erich Lessing/Musée du Louvre, Paris; **60** Scala/HIP; **61** Scala/Museo di Villa Giulia, Rome; **63** Art Archive/Dagli Orti/Heraklion Museum, Crete; **64** AKG/Erich Lessing/Musée du Louvre, Paris; **67** AKG/Erich Lessing/Kunsthistorisches Museum, Vienna; **69** Bridgeman Art Library/Victoria & Albert Museum; **70t** AKG/Rainer Hackenberg; **70b** Werner Forman Archive; **71t** AKG/Bildarchiv Monheim/Jochen Helle; **71b** Scala/Pompeii; **72** AKG/Erich Lessing/Museo Archeologico, Sperlonga; **73** Corbis/Fridmar Damn/zefa; **75** Bridgeman Art Library/Museum of Fine Arts, Boston; **76–77** Werner Forman Archive/British Museum; **78** Corbis/Araldo de Luca **81** AKG/Erich Lessing/Musée du Louvre, Paris; **82** Scala/Pushkin Museum, Moscow; **83** AKG/Erich Lessing/Vatican Museum; **84c** Werner Forman Archive/Museo Nazionale Romano, Rome; **84b** AKG/Erich Lessing/Israel Museum, Jerusalem; **85t** Art Archive/Dagli Orti/Museo Prenestino, Palestrina; **85b** Scala/Museo Pio-Clementino, Vatican; **87** Scala/Musei Capitolini, Rome; **88** AKG/Erich Lessing